Families Lost and Found

Families Lost and Found
Inspirational Stories of Genealogical Research

Compiled by
Lee Nelson
and
Marilyn Brown

CFI
Springville, Utah

ISBN: 1-55517-903-7
v.1

Published by CFI,
an imprint of Cedar Fort, Inc.
925 N. Main Springville, Utah, 84663
www.cedarfort.com

Distributed by:

Cover design by Nicole Williams
Cover design © 2005 by Lyle Mortimer

Printed in the United States of America
10 9 8 7 6 5 4 3 2 1

Printed on acid-free paper.

Contents

$\mathcal{P}$reface

by Lee Nelson

$\mathcal{O}$ver the years, we have published many stories about miracles. Some found their way into print in the *Beyond the Veil* series, which focused on near death experiences. We have published miraculous conversion stories, accounts of faith and priesthood blessings and healings, and all kinds of stories dealing with heavenly manifestations, personal inspiration, and revelations.

But in no field of study or area of interest are miracles more frequent or more commonplace than in the field of genealogical or family research. Corner any avid family researcher, ask for stories about miracles, and then stand back and be amazed. Pages in dusty vaults turn without the help of human hands; sought-after tombstones are seen in dreams; strangers suddenly appear to offer assistance without being asked; and dead ancestors regularly appear in dreams, or whisper into ears in an effort to offer needed guidance.

It's as if legions of departed spirits are crowded at the edge of the veil—whispering, shouting, nudging, tricking, inspiring—doing anything and everything with the means available to them to help the living join random names into family lines and groups.

In the late 1970s, while preparing to write my first historical novel, *The Storm Testament*, I attended a lecture by Alex Haley at Brigham Young University. His historical novel *Roots* had become an international best seller. But the invitation to speak at BYU had more to do with his genealogical research than being a successful novelist. In gathering research for his story, he had traced his family lines back to the plantations where his ancestors had been slaves, and even back to Africa, where they had been kidnapped into slavery. Haley's book *Roots* had glamorized genealogical research. It didn't seem fair that a novelist was getting all the glory for digging up a few names while true and dedicated genealogists with decades of hard work remained in the trenches, unrecognized and unrewarded, at least in the public eye.

Being somewhat of an opportunist by nature, I decided to join Alex Haley on the genealogy bandwagon. To kick off my series of historical novels, I wrote a prologue about a family history being mysteriously lost, then miraculously found. When the first *Storm Testament* volume was published, even though the copy on the jacket called it a historical novel, people began coming by my house, asking to see Dan Storm's lost journals. Others called on the phone, wanting to know why they couldn't find Dan Storm's headstone in the American Fork cemetery. Because of this magical prologue with a genealogical theme, thousands thought these historical novels were true. I received invitations to speak at the meetings of historical and genealogical societies. Even though the genealogical material was fiction, the Spirit of Elijah was one of the most powerful features in the story, representing its influence in turning the hearts of the children to the fathers.

Elijah is the prophet described in the book of Kings. He called down fire from heaven in an effort to turn people from Baal worship to the true god of Israel. Instead of tasting death, Elijah was taken to heaven in a fiery chariot. We don't know a lot about Elijah because he never wrote his own book. At least there is no book with his name on it in the Old Testament.

The final verse in the Old Testament, the last verse of Malachi, describes God's mandate to Elijah and his mission to us mortals, conducted from his place of residence in the world of spirits:

> *And he [Elijah] shall turn the heart of the fathers to the children, and the heart of the children to their fathers, lest I come and smite the earth with a curse.* (Malachi 4:6)

The world is cursed if people—past and present—are not connected in families and family lines. And so, legions of genealogists find and sort and bind individuals and families from generation to generation while Elijah and his hosts of angels help as much as possible to see this work accomplished.

Marilyn Brown and I decided one winter afternoon that maybe we could play a role in helping people become more aware of the miraculous work taking place in family research. We decided that we would publish some of the amazing stories we were hearing. Marilyn came up with the title *Families Lost and Found*. We sent out invitations, and stories started pouring in—heartwarming, inspiring, and many times miraculous.

We invite readers who didn't submit stories for this first volume to submit stories for future volumes. The authors of stories selected for publication will receive free copies of the published work. Send stories to *Families Lost and Found*, Box 531, Springville, Utah 84663, or e-mail submissions to authorleenelson@msn.com.

$\mathcal{I}$ntroduction
Help from the Other Side
by Marilyn Brown

$\mathcal{W}$hile I was busy cheering at high school football games, designing posters for proms, writing research papers, and eating peanut butter sandwiches for lunch, my mother—when she could take time from raising four active children—was busy doing genealogy.

I thought she looked hassled. I never asked her about what she was doing. And I'm sorry now. I could have learned a lot if I had asked her some questions.

However, it was usual for her to expect no questions. She was willing to share her experiences with my father, or a woman in Church who seemed interested. "I had a dream. I saw Priscilla. She stood above my bed and I knew without asking her where I could find those records. And there they were."

This kind of thing happened—oh, not every day—but enough that I grew up acquainted with the miracles that happen to family researchers. Though these experiences might have become commonplace, they were never ordinary. They were always an inspiration to me.

When I began looking for stories for this book (several came from the *Ensign*) and when people sent their stories to Cedar Fort, I was not at all surprised to read about the miracles that happened over and over again. Someone pulls the books out so that they are prominently displayed when the genealogist needs them; a researcher opens the book to the very page, or gets through to the correct film, or finds a note in the margin; an ancestor—or someone—appears in a dream; a researcher finds the gravestone in a place they had already looked many times before. Though I am never surprised at what I read, I am always overcome with gratitude for the communication our two worlds share.

Genealogical work is obviously supported from our loved ones on the other side. Every precious moment we spend looking—even if we do not find what we are looking for—will honor our ancestors with our dedication, our love, and our devotion. And then, someday, just when we expect it least, we might receive a payment with the sudden appearance of that one connection—as though it has been provided by a spirit ancestor who, for a long time, has been trying to get through.

Genealogy is a necessary work, sometimes a relentless work, but always a blessed work.

It is from those dedicated, hardworking researchers who are willing to do this work that these miraculous stories have come.

They are stories that will touch your heart and build your testimony. They are amazing, tender, priceless, and inspirational. Enjoy reading these stories of men and women who live on the edge of the world we will all someday enter. Someday we ourselves may be asking our own descendants for this same kind of help.

If you have a story for our next volume, please send it to the addresses Lee Nelson has indicated. We appreciate your sharing these miracles so all of us can enlarge our own experiences and testimonies.

Another Sister

by Dorothy Jacobs McMeen

My maternal grandfather's first child was a little girl born in the Great Smoky Mountains of Tennessee. They called her Bessie, though her given name was Elizabeth.

This grandfather, "Doc" Nahlon, at the time of Bessie's birth, was married to Sarah Ann Law. But the marriage did not last. Though he went on to raise many children in his second marriage with my maternal grandmother, he would often tell his family about their half sister, a little girl he had lost track of and had never known. He often wondered how she was doing, where she was, what she looked like now.

My mother, Mary Elisabeth Naillon, was impressed with her father's story about her half sister, Bessie. Though only seventeen when she married Carl Jacobs on July 26, 1921, and busy rearing their seven lively children, it was still her dream to visit those Smoky Mountains in eastern Tennessee to find her father's first home and perhaps be lucky enough to find her half sister.

As we children grew, my mother introduced us to genealogical research. We'd spend our Sunday afternoons writing letters or our personal histories. Each week we sent an inquiring letter to county records offices, genealogical societies, and/or other interested parties. All of us children became avid genealogists.

One morning in early 1950, a letter came to my mother, Mary, from a woman who said that her name was Elisabeth McNahlon, Bessie for short. She lived in North Carolina, although she had been born in Naillontown, Tennessee. Bessie said her parents had divorced when she was only two years old. Her father had gone west against her mother's wishes, and he had disappeared from their lives. She said her father's name was spelled Doc McNahlon. My mother's father was Doctor Lafayette Naillon. When my mother and this Bessie compared the records of the fathers of these two men, the name for both was Elijah Washington Naillon. This Elijah had fought for the Confederacy during the Civil War and established Naillontown in Cocke County, Tennessee. His son was the same Doc they knew as their father. Someone had changed the spelling of the name.

My mother had found her Bessie! This was a moment of absolute joy for her. As soon as she could make arrangements, she boarded a Greyhound bus and rode 2,536 miles to Gastonia, North Carolina, where Bessie lived. Bessie was there to meet her at the station. The two women looked at one another and then fell into each other's arms, tears in their eyes.

When they got to Bessie's house, my mother, Mary, commented that there was no question that she had found a relative. Bessie and her daughters favored the Naillon side. They were tall and lithe with reddish-blonde hair and light blue eyes. Bessie's three sons and Maude, Bessie's eldest daughter, also greeted Mary, their new aunt, with warmth. Jackie, Bessie's second daughter, arrived later to pick up Bessie for their night shift at the textile mill. After Mary's first night in the house, Bessie and all of her children woke her with kisses and hugs and excitement. They wanted her to stay with them forever.

Bessie told Mary that finding each other had sparked within her an entirely new energy for family research. She'd scoured public records and ancient cemeteries. She now believed that she knew the exact location of the land their forefathers had farmed. She was eager to take Mary with her to find out if the farm that she had discovered was the place their father had lived. She also hoped they could find information about some of their other relatives.

The next day, they drove wide highways through woodlands that gave way to verdant, shaded lanes. They found the Pigeon River and wound alongside its ribbonlike path. The traffic thinned as did the meandering roads. Now sturdy, weathered farmhouses stood against the landscape.

At last Bessie said, "I believe we're lost."

Mary woke from a reverie and suggested they stop to ask directions.

Just at that moment, a larger, once-white house came into view. It seemed rooted to the wide, red clearing. On the worn wraparound porch stood a young girl with brown braids. No fence defined the house from the wilderness. Scrappy chickens beat back the Virginia creeper vines.

My mother was reluctant to speak to the young girl, but she felt she ought to give it a try. "Good morning. My name is Mary Naillon Jacobs. Would your mother or father be home?"

Without a word, the child vanished behind the front door. Mary thought the child was shy and that they had seen the last of her. However, it was not long before a stern-browed woman came through the door, looking annoyed. The shy girl peered from behind her skirts.

"What fer ye?" the woman inquired, drying her hands on her apron.

"We are looking for a farm that was once owned by a family called Naillon. We know they farmed along this river. Do you know of any people by that name?"

"None 'round 'ere," she said. "This 'ere place has been in my husband's family fer nigh on fifty years. And all the land 'round it."

It was Bessie's turn to be brave. In her soft Southern drawl, she began to ask the woman about her farm, her family, and herself. They learned that her name was Luella Adair and her daughter's name was Selene.

"May I fetch ye a cup o' coffee?" Luella offered as she invited the researchers into her living room.

They accepted water and seated themselves on two of the four chairs around a centered table. The home was clean and neat, but it looked like there was no money. Everything in it looked as though it had had been made by hand.

3

From where my mother and Bessie were seated, their gaze traveled down the hallway to the back of the house. Along one wall was an old framed photograph. "Is that a picture of someone in your family?" Bessie asked.

"Oh no," replied Luella from the large kitchen. "That 'ere picture was 'ere when they bought this place. We jus' kep' it. Wasn't no bother."

Mary and Bessie looked at each other. Finally Mary spoke up again. "Would you mind if we looked at it more closely?"

It might have been bad manners, but both of the women got up from their places in the front room and walked down the narrow hallway. On the wall was a very interesting photograph in a wooden frame.

From the style of clothing worn by the subjects, the women knew it had been taken many years ago. They looked more closely at the familiar-looking young couple and the baby seated on its mother's lap. At once, Mary recognized her father's younger features. His hair was thicker and longer than she had known. At that same moment, Bessie saw her mother's eyes. The two women gaped in stunned silence.

Tenderly they removed the picture from the wall. On the back in a graceful hand was written "Sarah Ann Law with Bessie, May 4, 1898."

They carried it into the living room. Luella seemed surprised. We must assume that not every guest took pictures down from her wall.

"Do you know the party who owned this house before your family purchased it?" Mary asked.

The woman took a moment to think. "It was a man by the name of Lawson, Lawton, maybe Lawes, I'd be thinkin'," she replied.

Bessie breathlessly explained the photograph to Luella—this was a picture of Bessie when she was just a baby.

Luella seemed as elated as the two researchers were to have come upon such a treasure.

The women offered to purchase the photograph, but Luella

insisted that it was rightfully theirs. At Christmastime that year, the two sisters sent Luella another picture to fill the space on her wall.

Bessie and Mary copied the photograph so that all of their descendants could have this priceless picture of their father, but Bessie and her girls kept the original. The most precious find, my mother always insisted, was the farmhouse where her father had once lived, and a treasured friendship with her half sister, Bessie.

Find Iby

by Edwin Greenlaw Sapp

After I joined the Church, I was introduced to the exciting work of searching for my kindred dead. What could be more natural than to want to share with them what I now held sacred?

At one point I found myself searching for my mother's family, the Greenlaws—a family who left Scotland and settled in Maine.

My research ultimately brought me to the Daughters of the American Revolution (DAR) Constitution Hall in Washington, D.C., which is not far from my home in Maryland. The decision to look there changed my life—and the lives of several others—forever.

The night before my trip to Constitution Hall, I was waked from a sound sleep by a man's voice saying gently but insistently, "Find Iby." He pronounced the name "eye-bee." I awoke thinking someone was actually in the room, but since the voice had a calm tone and delivered a nonthreatening message, I wasn't afraid. I looked, saw no one, and concluded that I had just had a very realistic dream. Twice more that night, however, I awoke to the same voice urging me to "find Iby."

In the morning I discussed the unusual experience with my wife, Jeannie. There were no Greenlaws with that name, but after some thought, she recalled that the earliest recorded members of the Johnson family—her father's line—were Benjamin and Isabell, who was called "Iby."

I drove to Washington with the Greenlaws on my mind. I

knew that the head of the committee that planned the Johnson family reunion each year was a man who, for almost a quarter of a century, had served faithfully as clerk of court for Chatham County, North Carolina. During that time, he had combed all the courthouse records under his dominion for information that might lead to Ben and Iby's origins and their parents' names. Each year he had been forced to report that no new information had been found.

Accordingly, I had no illusions that the four hours I planned to spend looking at DAR records 350 miles away from Ben and Iby Johnson's home could reveal what twenty-five years of research with the original records had failed to find.

Consequently, I spent three and one half of the allotted four hours in total frustration, looking at records of what seemed to me to be the most prolific family in the early American Northeast. There were many complete Greenlaw families, but none were in my direct line.

Finally, the memory of that gentle voice came once more: "Find Iby."

With reluctance, awed by the monumental futility of the task, I went to the North Carolinas section and pulled at random a blue-covered typewritten manuscript from the shelf.

My heart sank when I realized what I held in my hands. The volume was a compilation of early wills on file at the Chatham County courthouse. What could be more useless! The data in that book had been collected from the indexes maintained and reviewed by the head of the Johnson family reunion—my wife's relative, the clerk of court for Chatham County.

In almost complete frustration, but still with a little half-hopeful prayer, I flipped open the book and stared at the page displayed. In that moment, several lives were changed forever.

On that page, before my eyes, the typewritten title of a misfiled document declared that what followed was the will of Samuel Gillmore. Samuel left property to his daughter Isabell, also known as "Iby," and to her husband, Benjamin Johnston (not Johnson) of Gulf.

Two little things—a misfiled will and a name change.

I had found Iby. I had found her because someone wanted her found. I had found her because I could help her. I had found her because the work of vicariously performing baptisms and other ordinances for the dead truly is a part of the plan of a loving Heavenly Father who wants us all to return to him.

"Find Iby," by Edwin Greenlaw Sapp.
Copyright Intellectual Reserve, Inc.
First published in the *Ensign*, July 1991.

Both Heaven and Earth

by Ron Bremer

*S*ome time ago, during the noon hour at the Ohio Genealogical Society annual convention, seven other women
were seated at the table where I was sitting. The lady straight
across from me said, "I am Catholic, but this genealogy is much
more than just a hobby. Strange things happen to me all the
time. Pages turn in the books that I am reading. I get these funny
hunches that prove very successful. I hear voices in the night.
And I often have dreams about my ancestors. It is as if genealogy
affects both heaven and earth."

I could only agree with her. "How true," I thought. And I
began to record many of the experiences I had heard from others
who had known that genealogy affects both heaven and earth.

* * *

While I was visiting the home of Mr. Warren G. Cantrell
of Killeen, Texas, he related the following story to me. He said
that he was a young man when he became interested in his family
genealogy. After a while, it became his life's work. So much so
that he decided to make a visit to DeKalb County, Tennessee,
where his research indicated his ancestors had resided.

The area was beautiful, leading to a wooded valley. He spotted an old house and drove up to see if anyone there knew anything about the Cantrells.

As he was closing his car door, a barefoot lady in a dress
stepped out onto her porch. "Where have you been? Everyone in
this valley is a Cantrell descendant, and exactly thirty years ago

we all had the same dream—that you would drive up here like you just did."

He was taken back and couldn't speak. He was quiet as he listened to what she had to say.

"So in preparation for this event, we all gathered together our old family records, Bibles, documents, pictures, stories, and many artifacts, and put them in this old trunk here on this porch. They have been here now for thirty years."

He was not sure whether he should shout for joy or apologize. But one thing was sure—he was still speechless.

"We knew that you would show up someday, but we never knew when," the woman said.

By this time, both she and Mr. Cantrell were in tears. They embraced one another for a long moment, and she invited him into the house. She called the rest of the relatives and told them to come over right away because "the man in our dreams has finally arrived."

* * *

After a seminar in Montana, I was the houseguest of one of the ladies I had spoken to. After dinner, she said, "May I ask you just one question about my grandfather, Henry Gabelbauer?"

"Certainly," I said.

She began to describe to me in great detail all the research she had done on this German ancestor who had immigrated to Milwaukee, Wisconsin. I offered her several suggestions.

The next morning, as we met for breakfast, I asked her how she had slept. I was surprised to hear her say, "I did not sleep a wink all night."

As she continued, my eyes filled with tears.

"After I went to bed," she explained, "my grandfather appeared in my room at the foot of my bed and spent the night telling me why I could not find his genealogy." She finished with a smile of joy on her face. "I now know exactly where to search for his information, and I am absolutely thrilled."

* * *

Years ago, I was asked to give an all-day genealogical seminar in Leavenworth, Kansas. It was held in a convent. Evidently, it was a retirement home for priests and nuns.

There was a special spirit in this place that lasted the full day. At the close of the proceedings, in the way I complete all of my seminars, I shared some of my most memorable genealogical stories with the attendees.

A spirit of reverence settled over the entire group. It seemed that everyone present could relate to these stories. Most were in tears.

After the seminar was over, many of the nuns and priests came up to me and shared their own spiritual experiences that had happened to them in researching genealogy. I could not help but remember the lady's words: "Genealogy affects both heaven and earth." It was an event I'll never forget.

* * *

After a seminar in Lawton, Oklahoma, my host for the night related the following story to me.

A home economics teacher at the local high school was asked to attend an annual convention of home economics teachers to be held in her ancestral county in Illinois. She thought to herself that this was an opportunity of a lifetime. She would try to find any information she could about her ancestors who were buried there.

While everyone broke for the lunch hour, she headed—full of excitement—to the local cemetery to find her grandparents. However, when she drove her car into the graveyard, she could not believe how huge it was. Thousands of gravestones met her eyes—row after row after row.

Feeling a little discouraged and knowing how limited her time was, she nevertheless opened the car door to get out and begin her search. As a dedicated Baptist, she believed in the power of prayer. So she sincerely beseeched her Father in Heaven to help her in any way he could.

No sooner had she stepped out of the car when she heard her grandfather say, "I am over here, honey."

She had to walk a long way, but she was directed to his burial site. Her grandmother was buried right next to him.

After she had taken pictures of both of her grandparents' tombstones, another voice said, "I am over here, honey." This other voice directed her to the burial site of two of her great-grandparents. And the voice again directed her to the tombs of her other great-grandparents.

This was the most amazing thing that ever happened to her!

* * *

During a break at one of my seminars in Lebanon, Oregon, a widow came up to me and related the following experience. She was preparing for bed alone, as her husband had passed away many years ago. As she finished her prayers and reached up to turn out the light, her husband came running into her bedroom and said, "Honey, get up, we have company!"

Because her husband had been dead for many years, this alone was shock enough. However, she put on her robe and walked with him into the front room. When she came through the hallway, she stood aghast. Over one hundred people were crowded into the room, all dressed in white.

One of those in the lead stepped forward and said, "We are all ancestors of your departed husband." She felt her heart pounding as the man continued.

"You are the only person on earth who can do this great work. Will you please help us?" She did, and she still does!

* * *

A lady in Indianapolis, Indiana, told me that her grandfather died when she was ten years old. At that early age, she barely remembered attending his funeral and the burial services. Yet in her genealogical research, she was careful to include the grand-father she barely remembered.

Many years later, when she happened to be in the vicinity of the cemetery where her grandfather was buried, she wondered if she could possibly find his grave. As she drove, she took an eastern route out of the town for a few miles, trying to remember the direction.

Surprised at herself, she was able to locate the cemetery. After walking around for a while, she indeed found her grandfather's plot.

And to her amazement, standing beside the tombstone was the spirit of her grandfather! Tears were running down his cheeks as though he were thanking her for thinking of him, and thanking her for doing such wonderful work in genealogy.

* * *

When I was employed the Genealogical Society of Utah, I was asked to locate the old records for the city of New York. There were lots of current records, but not many of the very old records.

A lady in Long Island had sent me information on the possible location of some old records. So I went to the building in question, but I just did not seem to be able to locate any old records.

After looking for half the day, I decided to walk around this old but tall building. When I entered by another doorway, I noticed a doorbell on the wall.

When I pushed the doorbell, a voice immediately asked, "Who is it?"

I answered, and one of the panels in the wall opened up to a steep musty stairwell. It looked a little frightening, but I began to walk down the old, rusty metal stairs.

Soon I was in a sub-basement—a basement below the basement—which had been built in the mid-1800s. Now I knew why I had not found anything previously. There was a basement, but the oldest records were in this sub-basement.

Two boilermen met me with large flashlights. I was their first visitor in years. They told me to follow them to the old records. It was dusty and dirty, with water dripping everywhere. The walls were lined with old rusty cans of war rations, and there were rats scurrying about among the refuse on the floor.

After the men with the flashlights had beckoned me forward for what seemed like a very long way, we came to a huge open room supported by thick steel beams. It was in this room that I found the old records in question. Some of them went back to the Dutch period. We estimated that there were at least fifty tons of records in the great storage area.

My Mother and Genealogy

by Bela Petsco

My mother, not a member of the Church, was not what one would call an educated woman, but she was a voracious reader—a trait both my brother and I developed as children. My reading tastes favored mysteries and historical novels, and there were always plenty of those around the apartment—or in the neighborhood library.

My brother favored Westerns and science fiction; I am not certain where he obtained all those paperbacks, but his nose was usually buried in one for hours and hours. Even on car trips around the country, Lawrence would be hunched in his corner of the backseat behind our father, absorbed in a paperback. To this day, I doubt my brother can recall most of the wonderful places we have traveled to as a family, for being totally engrossed in one or another of his paperbacks.

Well, I mentioned that my mother wasn't educated because she did not truly understand genealogy and all it entails, but she supported my exploration of our family history. I had told her that the Church encouraged its members to work on their personal genealogies, and so I wanted to work on mine.

My mother was not only a Farkas through her mother, but I believe she was a *farkas*. The *farkas* were an ancient Magyar tribe, the original Hungarians—one of the oldest. And, anciently, the *farkas* were the shamans. Of course, there is no way of knowing if we are descended from that tribe, but there were times my mother certainly seemed to know things that could not logically be explained. Anyway, when I explained about families being

15

united for time and all eternity, she said, "Yes, that is right," and she offered any help she could to get me started.

Progress was slow those first years, but after returning from my mission, I drove with my mother to Plainview, Long Island, to view microfilms the Church had recently made of the parish registers in Kisvarda, the Hungarian town of my mother's ancestors. My mother said she would help with any translations, should we find any information. We knew names, but no marriage dates—just approximations.

Viewing microfilm is not easy. The images are faint, and viewing them can strain good eyes. My mother was blind in one eye and the good one was not in the best condition. It soon became obvious she could not continue looking at the microfilm with me, and I suggested she not try.

She continued sitting beside me, but stared off to the side at a blank wall. I continued rolling through the reel of film, searching for familiar surnames. After a few minutes, my mother said, "Stop." She was still looking off at the blank wall. She turned to me and said, "Go back." I turned back a page. She said, "More." I slowly rolled back page by page until she said, "Stop." And she put her finger on the screen and said, "There." I looked where her finger pointed. It was the marriage entry for her parents. I had missed it completely while scanning the film. And from that one entry—and a few years' work—I was able to trace our entire Farkas line, and later, our entire Bodi line.

She had no explanation of how she had found that entry. She was just happy knowing that the family had been found.

Through the years, as I continued gathering information, one difficulty continued to plague me: my mother's brother, Istvan. My mother's parents had married in Hungary and had had two children there, Anna and Istvan. It was probably Great-grandfather Farkas, who first came to New York. Then my mother's father immigrated. Then my mother's mother came, leaving in Hungary my great-grandmother Farkas, Anna, and Istvan.

The three here worked to get the passage money to bring the last three to New York, only Istvan died in Hungary—at age six. Great-grandmother Farkas and Anna came alone. We have a photograph of Istvan's grave and grave marker, but a wreath hides the part of the marker where a date might be. According to law, the microfilming had to stop with 1895, and Istvan was born after 1895. Without an exact date, Istvan could only be an approximation in the genealogy record. This bothered my mother. She wanted him clearly united with the rest of the family.

Then, in the late 1960s, my mother began having these "dreams." They occurred only when she was alone at night when my father was away on business. She would be asleep and would feel something brushing against her face that would awaken her. It looked like a tree beside her bed, so she reached for her eyeglasses and put them on. The tree would then come into focus and she could see that it was a willow with the branches hanging over her bed. Standing by the trunk of the tree was a man dressed in white, looking as if he wanted to talk with her. So my mother let out a scream, and the tree and the man in white disappeared. Certain that what she had seen had gone, she took off her glasses and went back to sleep.

She did not relate this to me until maybe the second or third time she experienced it. I told her it was something good and if it happened again to ask the man what he wanted. She told me I was crazy if I thought she was going to start talking to it. She said, "If he started talking to me, I'd drop dead from a heart attack."

I insisted that it was something good. I said, "It is either your first baby or your brother. Ask him what he wants."

She said, "No." And she stuck to her decision—even though the dream recurred several times, again and again.

I became convinced that the man in white by the willow tree was her brother rather than my mother's first baby. Her brother was the only member of her immediate family whom we could not verify with a date and unite with the immediate family. Since she was adamant about not asking him what he wanted, I knew that to solve the mystery it would be necessary for me to go to Hungary, where I could perhaps find the grave in the photograph.

17

And perhaps there on that grave marker I could find the birth and death date for Uncle Istvan.

One night after I had left to do the research in Hungary, my mother had an amazing dream that she and I were walking in the cemetery in Kisvarda in weeds up to our waists, wet to the skin with dew. After hunting for what seemed like ages in her dream, we found her brother's grave, which made her so happy she began crying. At this point, she woke up and noticed what time it was. It was too early to get up, so she turned over and went back to sleep. She also noticed how contented and elated she felt after the dream. The next morning on the phone, she excitedly told Pauline Pasternak about her dream. Pauline suggested that she ought to make a record of the dream, including the time she had suddenly come awake.

Kisvarda, in the far northeast of Hungary, seems little changed in a hundred years. Now there are paved roads, electric wiring, and a few motor vehicles. In a nearby town, I had to wait while a child herded geese. Horses pulled wagons of hay that had been hand cut in the fields. The Kisvarda Catholic and Reformed churches were closed and locked. Hungary was then a Communist country. There are two Jewish cemeteries and one Christian cemetery. The Christian cemetery is divided by a path. Catholics are buried on one side with ornate crosses, and members of the Reformed church on the other with plain, austere crosses. A neatly kept section was full of newer headstones. The section I needed to search was overgrown with weeds—weeds three and four feet high. I waded in, a copy of the photo of Istvan's gravestone in my pocket.

The trek around the graveyard seemed impossible, tiring, and fruitless. I was anything but happy. There were some trees along the path that separated the Catholics from the Reformed, and under one tree was a bench. I sat a while on that bench, resting. I had been wading through weeds wet with dew, and my leather shoes were soaked. *All this way. All for naught,* I thought. And I then heard in my mind, "Go to Nyireghhaza." I stopped for a moment, hesitating. But I heard, "Go to Nyiregyhaza," as clearly as though someone had spoken to me.

I stood and started for my rented car to go to Nyiregyhaza. Where I was supposed to go in that large city, I was not certain. But off I headed. As I walked back through the section lined with the newer headstones, I could see that many of them had carvings of willow trees—obviously a Hungarian symbol for death and grieving. Only then did I remember we had a willow carved on Grandpa and Grandma Farkas's headstone.

In Nyiregyhaza, I went to the county archives. It was here that I found both my mother's brother's birth and death dates, as well as the documentation for several hundred other relatives—all names that have now been processed and added to our family records.

When I returned to New York, my mother told me the dream she had about the two of us searching through tall, dew-wet weeds for her brother's grave in Kisvarda. She showed me the date and time of the dream she had carefully recorded. The date was the day I was in the Kisvarda cemetery. The time—given the six hours difference in time between Hungary and New York—was the same.

After that, the willow tree with the man in white standing beside it never appeared to my mother again.

A Clue in an Obituary

by Carole M. Bethke Wright

*I*n 1999, I decided to begin in earnest to locate the siblings and parents of my father's grandmother, Mathilda. All I knew about Mathilda was that she was born in 1847 in Germany, and that she came to this country in 1884. I knew that her husband had come a year earlier from Gross Schoenfeld, Pommem, Germany, to Mayville, Wisconsin, to establish a home and find a job before he sent for his family, and that she came with four of her six children. But I had no idea who the couple's brothers and sisters were, and I knew nothing about their parents.

However, I had in my possession three pictures of Mathilda, and an obituary, which described her as a kind, compassionate, and lovely neighbor. The only clue in the obituary that might be of any help to me was in the last line. After reading all the names of those who attended the funeral, I found this at the very end: "And a sister, Albertine, from Steele, North Dakota."

I had spent years wondering if I could do anything with this clue—that she had a sister named Albertine. If I could find Albertine, could I find her other siblings, and their parents?

I moved from Wisconsin to Provo, Utah, in 1995, and then I had access to the genealogical library. One day, I opened a drawer of state census microfilm from North Dakota. Amongst the boxes was a Steele County listing. I thought to myself, *That must be what the obituary meant—that she was from Steele County, North Dakota.*

Luckily Albertine was an unusual name. However, since I did not have a surname, I would have to go through every house listing in the county looking for the name Albertine.

Since I knew that Mathilda was born in 1847, I surmised that her sister's birth date was close to that year. I started with the 1880 census because I thought that she would probably have been in North Dakota by then.

At first I found only one Albertine in the whole county, but I knew that she was not the person I was looking for because she was much too old. I turned to the 1900 Census, and found one or two Albertines, but they were children.

Taking a good-sized pillow to sit on, I continued day after day, spending often eight hours slowly plodding through the towns on the films. I went through the 1905, 1910, and 1920 films. By this time, I was puzzled. Where could she be?

One day, I decided to call the libraries up in North Dakota. One of the librarians told me that Steele was not only a county, but also the name of a town in Kidder County, North Dakota. The obituary had said "Steele, North Dakota." I got excited. Perhaps Steele was the town instead of the county. I had been looking in the wrong county! I began looking through all of the names in Kidder County for the year 1880. I found a couple of Albertines, but nothing concrete. I was pretty discouraged, so I decided to do other things for a while.

However, I thought, "I'll try just once more before I quit completely." And amazingly when I got to the 1900 film, something exciting happened! When I looked through the Woodlawn Township of Kidder County, my eye caught on the very last entry of the list. I saw the name Bethke. Above the name was a scribble in black ink with a line drawn through it, making it barely readable: it looked like Brasch, Albertine.

I could not read the first word, so I might have dismissed this Albertine. However, beneath her name was the name of Bethke, Herman.

I was stunned. This was my grandfather, Herman Bethke! Here he was, listed as a young man at the age of twenty-four as Albertine's nephew!

And there was more. Beneath Herman's name was the name

Lorimer, Annie and Bruce M. I knew that Annie Bethke was my grandfather's sister. She had married a Lorimer, and Bruce M. was a little boy at the time, only three years old.

The name of Herman Wiesenhutter, age thirty-four, was also listed; he was a boarder of some relation to Albertine, or related to her former husband, because ten years later she willed her farm and property to him and his sister.

I had found our long-lost great-aunt Albertine!

After I sent away for whatever records were available in Kidder County on the family, I discovered that she had come to America in 1885, one year after her sister Mathilda. She had married John Brasch, who had died sometime before this census. While Mathilda ended up in Wisconsin, Albertine had ended up in North Dakota.

The census taker of June 5, 1900, a J. A. Marsh, told us from his records that Albertine was a Caucasian widow, born in Germany in September of 1848, and was fifty-one years old when the census was taken.

Though I realized I would need to continue my research to discover the parents' names, I was thrilled to have discovered Aunt Albertine.

The miracle in my discovery was that my young grandfather Herman Bethke and his sister Annie Lorimer did not really belong in this household when the census taker came! They were both from Milwaukee, Wisconsin, and just happened to be visiting their Aunt Albertine at the time that Mr. Marsh had come by their home to take the census. I always wondered if some higher power planned this visit so that I would be able to find this great-aunt at this time.

Inspired by a Wisecrack

by Lola Frances Murphy McMeen

When I was a child in Jasper County, Iowa, during the early 1900s, we sometimes went to visit my grandfather Daniel Washington Murphy who lived about twenty-five miles away on a farm in the Buena Vista Township.

We didn't go often to visit because we did not have a car and twenty-five miles was a long way to go in the surrey. But we loved to visit my grandfather, who lived in his rambling farmhouse with his unmarried daughter Hermea, and his two youngest sons, Hugh and Olin.

Grandfather Daniel's home was not the only house on the property. In the front of the farmyard was a very small pioneer home where grandfather's bachelor brother Townsend Murphy lived. We were sometimes able to visit with Uncle Townsend, but the visits were always in Grandfather Daniel's house. We never walked into our uncle's house. I was so young that I didn't know the difference, and I still can't remember my father's uncle well.

However, I vividly remember when he died. Mother and Father were sad about his death. Knowing that my grandfather would also be sad, they decided to visit the farm to comfort him. It was on this visit that we were first allowed to walk into Uncle Townsend's house. It was crowded with his belongings. I can vividly remember looking around the room at all the things he had so carefully saved. There were some of the most interesting relics I had ever seen—old china, silverware, and yellowing bits of paper and postcards. Grandfather may have given us some of these objects, but I can't remember much about anything else except

23

one particular old sheaf of bound pages that looked like a book.

It was a precious old book that my grandfather Daniel Washington Murphy gave to my father, Ashel Murphy, and it became a unique treasure of inspiration to me. It was a handwritten volume with dates and accounts and pages and pages of what looked like records.

At first I didn't think much about the book. I was much too young to appreciate musty old things. However, when we got home, as a source of entertainment in the evenings my father began reading from the pages of the book as we sat around the dinner table. The stories he read about my ancestors were fascinating. There were stories about our Murphy ancestors—one was about the mid-seventeenth century Hugh O'Murphy of the Royal Family of O'Morcho seated in County Wexford in southern Ireland, who educated his son John for the Roman Catholic Priesthood. The story became interesting when it told of John falling in love with a redheaded Scottish girl named Mary Campbell and joining the Church of England. For this infraction, his father disowned him. However, a Lord Hillsboro gave him a lease on fourteen acres of land where he settled, became an auctioneer, and collected tolls on the king's highway. Since he was no longer nobility, he dropped the prefix "O" from his name and became John Murphy. "These are our ancestors?" I wanted to know. "Yes," my father assured me. All of this fascinated me.

Though I can't remember the details of many of the stories now, I do remember how we as children were awed by one particular entry that impressed us in a strange way. Uncle Townsend had written about one of the children as, "Rebecca who was sensible and died in infancy." She was sensible when she died in infancy? I and my brothers and sisters really thought about that one. That one example of his dry sense of humor resonated in my mind for years, and I never forgot it.

Some thirty years from this time, after I converted to The Church of Jesus Christ of Latter-day Saints, I discovered another small book containing the material from Uncle Townsend's book, and other material that had been printed in 1905 in Jasper County under the auspices of Grandfather's brother, John Murphy. These two sources instilled a desire in me to know about my ancestors. From this point on, one inspirational thing after another happened to me. In my hundreds of trips to cemeteries, libraries, and courthouses, I experienced miracles that were explainable only as the help of the Spirit.

At one time, knowing that I would not be in Indiana again, I begged an irate librarian at closing time to let me find a critical book. After I said a silent prayer, I was able to slip through the door, and miraculously I was led to the book immediately. Similar events happened at other times, and miracles also happened in the cemeteries. Once I looked through the stones in a cemetery until almost dusk, when I found the gravestone I was looking for. Once one of the visitors to the genealogical library told me, "A person in white is standing behind every researcher in the genealogy library." I know that this is true.

I Found a Hero

by Ryan Jones

*B*ecause my mother's father died when she was only nine, the only grandfather I have ever known was my step-grandfather, Frank.

However, in about 1998, I grew curious to find out more about my biological grandfather on my mother's line, Grandfather Rose. My grandmother Irene knew his death date but was unsure of where he was born. She didn't know much about his family. I wanted to know as much as I could, so I began the long process of trying to discover his records.

At first I checked the Family History Center in Payson, but I didn't find much, so I went to the records at BYU. I discovered that William's father was a miner in Eureka and was from Sweden. I also discovered that all of his temple work had been done. So now that I knew that someone was aware of my family members, I wanted to know who it was. In the BYU records I learned that a Mr. Val Kilpack had sent in the names on the Rose side of the family.

I didn't know where Val Kilpack lived, or what his phone number might be, but I suspected that someone in the Utah County area might have heard of him.

After looking around, I called Information and asked them to search for him. They found a Kilpack, and when I called him, I discovered he was indeed the same man who had sent in the names. Excited, I made an appointment to talk to him. It just happened to be a few days before Mother's Day. I had decided I wanted to present this research about my grandfather to my

26

grandmother as a Mother's Day gift.

The next day when I drove to Orem, I arrived at his house feeling a little like a total stranger who might be an imposition. After I knocked on the door, he answered and invited me in. The house was beautiful. Beautiful paintings hung on all the walls around me. The smell of Sunday dinner was still fresh in the air. I could tell that he was an educated man—his library was huge. He was a retired older man who seemed wise and gentle. He invited me into his office, where he had a CD that he had prepared for me. As we talked he shared a great deal of information with me. He explained that there were more than eleven thousand names and over thirty-five photos of my grandparents!

After our meeting, I rushed home, excited to go over the new information. After merging the data, I searched through the names as if traveling back through time. Many of my ancestors were indeed kings and emperors; others were just regular people. But the story that most interested me was one about my great-grandfather, Alvin Rose, and how he was converted to the Church. It was in my discovery of this remarkable great-grandfather that I found a hero.

Great-grandfather Alvin Rose, who was not a Mormon Pioneer, nevertheless came to Utah and established one of the greatest mines in Eureka, Utah. Later he lost the mine and was left without an occupation. So he began to deliver mining equipment to Montana.

One year, as he traveled back from Montana through Idaho, he came upon a field strewn with the bodies of Indian men and women. It was a horrible scene. He later learned that this massacre had occurred three days before he had arrived at this place. With anxiety and trepidation, Alvin Rose got down off the wagon to check the bodies, hoping he could find some of them still alive. He was aware that there could have been Indians watching him.

Nervously, as he looked around, he heard a baby crying. Following the cry, he came upon a woman lying in the grass among the other bodies. There was a large hump under the blanket on her back, and he could hear the baby crying.

Quickly he went to the woman with the lumpy blanket on her back. Though she was dead, the tiny baby girl in the papoose cradle was still alive! Alarmed, he took the little baby in his arms. Holding her close, he calmed her cries and took her with him back to the wagon. At once he loved the baby. As he traveled back to Utah with her, he realized he was not able to give her what she needed. When she cried for milk, he had no way to satisfy her hunger. As he passed through Ogden, his thoughts raced. He was trying to think of someone who might take the little girl. He thought of an LDS family who had been his friends.

Not really wanting to part with the baby, but knowing what was best for her, my great-grandfather gave her to this family. These parents and their children rejoiced. They adopted the Indian girl, named her Ann, gave her a proper home, and raised her to a lovely young woman.

This was not the end of Great-grandfather Rose's relationship with the girl.

Every time he took mining equipment to Montana, he stopped in Ogden to see Ann. Ann loved to see him, and they were close friends. However, as the little girl grew older, my great-grandfather became too old to travel. As he settled down in the Eureka area, he didn't get to Ogden anymore. Ann lost track of the man who had saved her life. But as an adult she did not forget him. After looking for him for several years, she finally tracked him down. When she found him in Eureka and reminded him of who she was, he was so amazed and grateful that he sat and listened to everything she had to say. He was still not a member of the Church. So during one of her visits, she gave him a Book of Mormon. She told him that she knew that it was true. She had a powerful testimony of The Church of Jesus Christ of Latter-day Saints. With a glad heart Ann taught him the gospel.

Great-grandfather Rose was baptized just weeks before he died.

Though I have not been able to place Ann in my research, the discovery of the compassionate character of this great-grandfather was priceless to me. Later I was able to give this information to my mother for Mother's Day. Her present also contained pictures, and among them was the picture of my great-grandfather. He became a hero to both of us. I want to be more like him.

We are all on a journey, and as we go we leave good or bad. Our actions and histories stand as an example to others; others can look upon our works as a source of hope. We can look to the past to give ourselves direction in future choices we will make. In turn, these paths in life stand as a monument to our character. I understand how our choices in life determine how we are remembered for generations.

A Name in a Dream

by Eunice Polatis

*I*t has been the custom in our family for each parent to select a name for the unborn child. In those days, we never knew if it was a boy or a girl until birth. Well, when I was about six months along, Dean woke me up early one morning and said, "If this is a boy, his name should be DuRo."

My question to him was, "Why DuRo?" I thought, *What a strange name.*

He told me that he had dreamed about a soldier who was so brave and such a great warrior that even the enemy respected him. His name was DuRo.

Well, I began to pray in earnest for a girl this time. I thought it would be awful to name a baby DuRo. When the baby was born five weeks early, and I was told that it was a boy, my heart sank. My very first thought was, *Oh no! This kid has to be named DuRo.*

I prevailed, however, by giving him the first name of my choice—Logan. But yes, his middle name became DuRo.

When Logan DuRo Polatis was about three years old, our family held a meeting at Grandma's home in Thomas, Idaho. At this meeting, Lowell Thomas announced that he had finally come across a line through Mother's side that he had not ever seen before, and the name was DuRoe, or Duroe.

When he made this announcement, and told us how it was spelled, Dean said, "We spell ours DuRo."

Lowell said, "What do you mean 'ours'?"

Dean replied, "We have a son named DuRo."

Lowell asked us where we got the name, and Dean told him that he dreamed it. Later I asked Dean why he didn't spell it correctly, and he said, "I don't dream in writing, just in talking."

Catching a Big Fish

by Carole M. Bethke Wright

I often felt that doing genealogical research was a lot like fishing. You get a nibble or two and that entices you to try harder. Then you get a bite, and *wow*, you're really onto the big one now! When you hit the jackpot, or pull in the big one, it's ecstasy for a week or more.

My aunt Rosie and I often did genealogical research together. One day she told me about an old schoolhouse up in Manitowoc, Wisconsin. It was now being renovated. She believed there were old records of the Manitowoc Historical Society somewhere in that old school.

I called her from my home in West Bend, Wisconsin, and asked how we could get into the old building. She said she would contact Mr. Ed Ehlert, who had the key. Luckily, he was happy to open it for us. I drove up to Manitowoc early on the next warm June morning.

Faithful Aunt Rosie was standing at the doorway of the school waiting for me. When we went into the old building, it seemed stuffy. But it was clean. Boxes stood piled high all over in the room. I remember old plaster dummies sporting clothing from another century, and there were various old military uniforms hanging about.

Our goal that day was to find a marriage record we had never found. We knew that our pioneer ancestor Anna Kellner and her husband, Samuel Williams, were married in Canada and had moved to Manitowoc, Wisconsin, where they had established themselves in the hotel business.

When Rosie and I saw all the boxes, Rosie stood still for a minute with a long face. "Where should we begin?" she asked. All day we opened boxes—sorting, peeking, and digging into this one and that. As late afternoon arrived, I felt dusty and hot, perspiring in my white outfit, and I had the distinct feeling we were looking in the wrong place. I reminded Rosie that Mr. Ehlert had called down the hall earlier to tell us that he would be closing the building at four o'clock. We were almost finished, so we decided to look a little faster.

With just three boxes to go, I weakened and said, "Let's let them go. The record surely is not here at this site."

Rosie looked at me and said, "Oh, no! We still have these three boxes to do and there are still a few minutes left."

I hesitated, fussing a little because I was feeling hot and dusty. But with her encouragement, I dug into the project again. When I opened the top box, I found another box of business ledgers. We had come across many old business ledgers that day from old businesses that had not destroyed their ledgers when they went out of business, but had given them to the historical society just in case they were useful. Many of the ledgers we had opened that day belonged to businesses owned by our Kellner ancestors. These people were merchants, but their records were really of no use to us now. The second box was just as uninteresting as I flipped through each ledger just to make sure there were no surprises hiding inside.

Finally, we were at the bottom box. It had only two ledgers in it. The top one had never been written in. I passed it to Rosie to hold while I reached in to examine the bottom one. It looked almost the same as the first ledger, but as I flipped the hard cover open, there was a piece of typed paper lying between the cover and the pages. I looked at it for a second. Some of it was written in French. As I peered intently at the letters, I saw the names "Annie Kellner and Samuel Williams." Softly I exclaimed, "Rosie! I think this is it!"

It was indeed the marriage record of Annie and Samuel. Rosie looked closer, and sure enough, the date and time and place said it all. We stared at each other for a long time with Cheshire Cat smiles, until I thought our faces would crack. We hugged each other and laughed and laughed, and hugged again. Then we told Mr. Ehlert, who had just walked through the door, that we had "caught the big one we had come for."

Mr. Ehlert smiled a broad smile and refrained from locking up until we could hurry to the print shop for copies. We hurried along, jabbering excitedly, not believing our good fortune.

When we returned, we placed the original record back where we found it in the ledger book where it had rested safely for over a hundred years. It was such a great feeling to know we finally had the information now to complete the Williamses' story. We drove home—actually it was more like flying home—feeling like we were on cloud nine because we had made such a great "catch."

What did I learn from this experience? Apparently something that Aunt Rosie had learned long ago: "Always hoe to the end of your row!"

The Faceless Man

by Catherine Ramognino Thorpe, as told to Don O. Thorpe

I was visiting my father in Cagnes-sur-Mer in the south of France, and he was showing me photographs of my relatives in an old, dusty album.

As we came to a faded group photo with a man's face cut out of it, I stopped him from turning the page. "Who was that?" I asked.

"My grandfather, your great-grandfather," he replied. He looked off into the distance and shook his head. "I'm sorry to say I don't know much about him—I don't know what he looked like, and I don't even know his first name."

Although my father's last name, Ramognino, is Italian, he was born in France, as I was. I had lived in the heart of Paris for the first twenty-three years of my life. So it was with interest that I asked about this faceless man, my great-grandfather, who was Italian.

My grandfather had cut the face out of the photograph because he hated my great-grandfather for leaving his family. Up to the day he died, several months before I looked in the album, my grandfather refused to say anything about this man to his children.

Father told me as much as he knew; my great-grandfather was a native of northern Italy and had immigrated to France as a young man, married a beautiful young French girl, and had three sons. Then one day he left his home and family, never to return. No one knows why, and no one knows where he went. His broken-hearted sons, especially my grandfather, grew up resenting their father.

Though Dad had tried to find his grandfather, his efforts were in vain. Relatives mentioned that he had blue eyes and had been quite tall—six feet seven inches—which was particularly unusual for an Italian. On two occasions, forty years earlier, my father had learned that a "tall Italian" had been in the area and had inquired about him. Later he became convinced that the man must have been his grandfather.

I left France that year feeling a little sad because my father never even had a chance to see his grandfather. I was determined to do all I could to find him myself.

This was difficult, however, because all the people connected with him had either died or refused to say anything about him.

Ironically, I was able to learn my great-grandfather's full name because of my grandfather's death. I knew my grandfather's death certificate would have my great-grandfather's full name on it, but I didn't know which district in Paris would have the certificate on file. There are twenty districts in Paris, and though it seemed like an arduous task, I began the search. I wrote to all twenty district courthouses asking if they had the death certificate, but I received negative responses from all of them. I decided to visit each one personally the next time I went to France in case a clerk had been careless.

Several years later, when I went to Paris to visit relatives, I continued the search for my great-grandfather. I traveled six hundred miles from Paris to interview my father again, and this time he seemed to think my grandfather had died in the fifteenth district. But that district had already replied negatively to my written request. So I returned to Paris and, with some reluctance, decided to go to the fifteenth district courthouse. I didn't expect to find anything because I had already visited several other courthouses with no success.

While my husband photographed a small park nearby, I went inside the building. Minutes later I rushed outside and ran down the steps, waving a piece of paper. "I found him, I found him!" I shouted to Don. "His name is Nicolas—Nicolas Ramognino!"

Later we felt my great-grandfather's presence in the temple

when my husband was baptized and confirmed for him. We felt so close to him we named our next son Stewart Nicolas. I still don't know the details of what happened to the faceless man in the photograph and why he left his family suddenly, never to be heard from again. But the spirit of the gospel, and my enthusiasm for finding my ancestors beyond the veil, has filled my heart with love for my great-grandfather. My husband and children value him as part of our eternal family, and we will always remember his name.

"The Faceless Man," by
Catherine Ramognino Thorpe and Don. O. Thorpe.
Copyright Intellectual Reserve, Inc.
First published in the *Ensign*, January 1998.

The Sound of the Bugle

by Lincoln Fuqua

$\mathscr{S}$ome loyal patriots I discovered in my line of ancestors were the talented American politicians, the Harrisons. The more recent Benjamin Harrison, the twenty-third president (1833-1901), was the grandson of the elder William Henry Harrison, the ninth president (1773-1841). The political heritage of the Harrison family began long before this; the grandfather of William Henry, Benjamin Harrison V (1726-1791), the fifth in a line of active politicians all bearing the same name, served as Speaker of the Virginia House of Burgesses, and was a member of the First Continental Congress. He chaired the committee that adopted the Declaration of Independence and was one of its signers. He also served three terms as governor of Virginia, and as speaker of the lower house of the state legislature.

Benjamin was a rotund, jovial man who loved luxury and had a taste for good food and wine. With his expansive personality, acquiring the nickname "Falstaff of Congress," he had been successful in amassing the Harrison family's wealth. He owned eight plantations and a ship building company. Perhaps not his most respected achievement, but one that stands out as a possible reason for his popularity, is that he began the first distillation of Bourbon whiskey. Members of our family took the recipe with them when they migrated to the Kentucky Territory after the Reveolutionary War. There they entered the distillery business—both legally and illegally—and made Kentucky Bourbon world famous. There are major distilleries in our hometown of Owensboro, Kentucky, to this day. During the Civil War—since

38

our property was only fifteen miles from the border between the North and the South along the Ohio River—our family's Westerfield Distillery provided "white lightening" for the troops of both sides so that they might endure the ravages of the war.

The long line of Harrisons were Southern gentleman planters and the generosity of Benjamin Harrison was one of the major factors in the success of the American Revolution. The family farm, the Berkeley Plantation, was a scene of battle in both the Revolutionary and Civil wars, and is honored in an annual celebration every Thanksgiving as a refuge for those heroes who trekked across its fields and for those hundreds of soldiers who died on its grounds. It was here also, during the American Revolution, that the song "Taps" was written and played to troops encamped on the property.

For several years I had been aware that a cemetery existed on the plantation, and I was hopeful that I could find it and record the names of this Benjamin Harrison's family and friends. With my many obligations, it was not possible for me to make repeat trips, so during a genealogical expedition several years ago I felt determined to find this cemetery before I had to leave for home.

Alone, I arrived at the Berkeley Plantation at sunset on a cold winter night in December when the grounds were covered with snow. No one else was on the property at this hour except for some wild geese eating the harvest's loose corn from the fall.

I toured the grounds until almost dark without finding the family cemetery that I felt compelled to seek out. Before I totally gave up in despair, I knelt down all alone under the darkening sky and asked for heavenly help. As I then arose and looked around one more time, I heard the faint sound of a bugle. I turned in the direction of that sound.

In the twilight I spotted a knoll in the distance crested by a clump of trees. Hopeful, I struck out across the snow in that direction. On the way, I walked past a monument where I could see a commemorative plaque. When I stopped to read it, my heart thumped in my chest. It told the story of how the song "Taps" was first played here during a Revolutionary War encampment.

To my surprise, just as it was beginning to get dark, I saw a group of headstones on the crest of this mound. I had found the family burial plot I had so desperately sought. On this knoll, I had a fabulous view out over the little harbor on the James River where the ships dock at the plantation for the annual Thanksgiving celebration. Here was the spot where the plantation's goods used to be loaded for shipping to market. As it was now dusk, I proceeded to flash-photograph all of the monuments in the graveyard so that I could extract the data to later process for performing the sacred temple ordinances for this prominent member of our family and his other close family and friends interred there.

I was so overcome with the spirit of gratitude for those who resided on the other side of the veil and for the help I had undoubtedly received from them. There was no question in my mind that they had interceded on my behalf in that moment I had heard the sound of the bugle. I knew that they were aware that I had traveled many thousands of miles from Utah on this errand in their behalf.

Finding Grandma Toth

by Patricia T. Barton

*T*hat's easy for them to say!" I muttered while mashing potatoes one Sunday after church.

With all my heart, I wanted to graduate from the family history class I was taking. And now it was impossible. Our Sunday School teacher had announced that afternoon: "In order to graduate from this class, you need to submit a family name and have it cleared for temple work. Our goal is to have this done in time to make a group trip to the temple this March."

There was no way I could find an ancestral name and have it cleared for temple work in just a few months. The research had already been done for generations back on most of my mother's lines. Any names with verifiable dates had already had their temple work performed.

"What about your dad's line?" asked my teacher. He was not as willing as I was to admit defeat.

But that was no help to me. My dad had joined the Church fifteen years earlier and he had soon found that any significant family history research was impossible.

I told my teacher, "My great-grandfather was an orphan in Hungary. All of our records are behind the Iron Curtain. My grandfather is nearly ninety, and his memory is no longer reliable."

Although my heart was no longer in it, I continued to attend the class. As the deadline for name submissions came nearer and the other students' enthusiasm grew, I was forced to reconsider. Maybe there was a possibility that I had overlooked.

One day an idea came to me like a thunderbolt: Grandma Toth! How could I have overlooked her? I made plans to write to my mother before the day was over, but I was so excited about the idea that I decided to phone her.

"Mom, this is Pat," I blurted out. "Has the temple work ever been done for Grandma Toth?"

There was a pause on the other end as my mother tried to think of an answer for this question that had come out of nowhere.

"No," she answered.

"Is there any reason why?" I demanded. "I mean, like the lack of documentation or dates or anything?"

Another pause. "No, I guess the only reason is that no one has ever thought of it before."

My heart raced as I explained the class, the assignment, and the deadline.

"I'll check things out and get back to you," Mom promised.

Grandma Toth was my dad's mother. She died when I was only eleven months old, so all I knew about her was what I had seen in a black and white snapshot. Now, twenty-four years later, we were about to be, in a way, introduced.

As my mother sent me certificates and passports, I pieced together the facts of Grandma Toth's life. Soon there was enough data to submit her name for temple work. The class deadline had long since passed, but I no longer cared. What had once been my sole motivation now vanished in the overwhelming joy and spirit of the work itself.

How easy it became! The name submission form was not the monster I had feared. The data was entered, checked, and sent on its way.

One day in early October a brown envelope arrived from the Church's Family History Department. With my fingers trembling and my eyes quickly clouding with tears, I tore the seal open. Yes! Yes! The name had been cleared and placed in the family file at the Provo Temple.

Now that my dream had become reality, I began to have doubts. Had Grandma Toth accepted the gospel? Would she accept the baptism? Was I doing the right thing?

Almost a year had passed since that frustrating Sunday afternoon in my family history class. The beautiful autumn sunshine glowed as I arrived in Provo. The temple workers guided me through the necessary preparations.

As we stood in the font, the young priesthood bearer who would perform the ordinance asked, "What relation is Mary Kerger Toth to you?"

"She's my grandmother."

"Finding Grandma Toth," by Patricia T. Barton.
Copyright Intellectual Reserve, Inc.
First published in the *Ensign,* April 1991.

Miracles Happen

by Steve and Deidrien Booth

*F*or as many years as computers have been available to keep track of genealogical research, Steve and Deidrien have put names in a special file on their hard drive. Thinking that they would someday get all of the material out, they had never backed it up on disks. As the files grew larger and larger, holding tens and thousands of names, they might have sometimes wondered if they should copy everything in case something might happen. But, like many of us who procrastinate for "just a little while longer," they held off copying the names to disks.

As luck would have it, the worst happened—the computer crashed. They were devastated. The names were lost. Both were stunned. For days, Deidrien was in tears. The research had represented years and years of work. And now it was gone.

As Steve's brother Mike came to rebuild the computer, they stood heartsick, watching his activities, knowing that no matter how well he fixed the computer, there would still be an emptiness that no amount of compassionate service, no technical knowledge, could remedy.

One morning when Steve was still in bed, Deidrien went to the rebuilt computer and thumbed through some papers on the desk. She found some items she had not seen before. As Steve lay sleeping, she found a floppy disk she had not known existed. She put it into the disk drive. The date of the backup was three days before the crash.

Shocked and excited, she ran through the contents of the floppy disk. All of the genealogy was there. She couldn't believe it. Waking Steve, she said, "Steve, you did back this up! It's still here!" Excited, she showed it to him.

Steve thought his heart would stop. "No, Deidrien. I did not back this up," he said.

The two of them looked at one another in amazement—and in pure joy. Miracles still happen. And this was one of them.

* * *

When Deidrien's grandfather was in his mideighties, she visited with him in his California home. There was one line in his ancestral files that she had never been able to find. She had gone through all of the motions. She had sent e-mails to hundreds of people. She had looked in hundreds of files and records in different cities. The line had come to a complete stop.

When she saw her grandfather, she knew that he would not be here much longer.

Earnestly, she pleaded with him, "Grandpa, I'm going to give you an assignment. When you get to the other side, I want you to help me to find a way to break through this line."

Her grandfather was very willing. He smiled at her and promised that he would.

"That's all I ask of you, Grandpa. That's your job."

Deidrien's grandfather died soon after that. Within a month of his death, one of the people Deidrien had e-mailed answered her and said, "Yes, I am related to these people, and I am connected to that line."

* * *

Deidrien's grandmother from Poland had left no records. As the first wife of her grandfather, very little was known of her. There were some brief bits of information, but one of Deidrien's cousins, who had been trying to search out the line, knew that some of the records were wrong.

One night, this cousin had a dream. In the dream, she saw a rock arch and under it, thousands of people reaching out to her.

It was not long after this dream that Deidrien and her cousin were able to take a trip to the Ukraine. Now they could look through some of the records that might reveal what had happened to their grandmother's people. They did not find anything while searching in the small town that had been indicated in the grandmother's records.

Discouraged at the end of the week, they finally decided on Sunday to attend Church before they took their flight home. At that meeting, they met a young Ukrainian man who had just been on a mission to Provo, Utah. Excited about meeting someone they knew from the States, someone who knew Utah Valley, they asked him if he could take them around to show them some features of the town that might help in their research. They told him they had been looking everywhere and hadn't come upon anything.

"Sure, I'll be happy to help you," the young missionary said.

As they walked with him, they realized how much more he knew about the town than they could ever have known. At one point—just out of the blue—he turned from the street and started down an alley they had not seen before. Deidrien's cousin stopped, taken aback. She was overcome with amazement. In front of her was a building with an arch. It was the arch she had seen in her dream.

They did not hesitate. "We'd like to go in that building," Deidrien told the missionary.

"Well, all right . . ." he said. He seemed a little reluctant to knock on any doors, but he was ready to help the women if he could.

An older lady came to the door. She barely opened it. If the missionary had not been there to explain to her who Deidrien and her cousin were, the woman would have would shut the door. She looked with a suspicious frown at the three visitors.

"We are in search of some records that you might have," the cousin had the missionary translate. She was going only on the strength of her dream. The woman shook her head. She had nothing, she told them.

But the visitors persisted. "Please help us. We have come all the way from Utah in America to search out our ancestors."

The woman looked at them with a stern look. "Utah?" she asked.

"Yes. We are from Utah."

After a moment passed, the woman opened the door a little more. "I just last week sent copies of all my books to Utah."

Deidrien thought the world would open up beneath her feet. "All your books?" she asked through the missionary.

"Yes. I do have some books that I have been taking care of through World War II." She stopped. "Are you LDS?"

"Yes, we are," Deidrien said enthusiastically. "May we please see your books?"

The woman invited them into her house and took them to a room where papers and books were piled on the desks. Miraculously, this was the woman who had been entrusted with records that the Polish courts feared would be destroyed in World War II. For years she had been secretly guarding the records of thousands and thousands of Polish people whose material would have been lost during the war. Graciously, she allowed Deidrien and her cousin full access to the material, where they found everything they needed and more. The arms of those who had reached up in the cousin's dream had finally found their benefactors. And the heavens had opened up to Deidrien and her cousin in a way that would never be forgotten.

Doors That Opened for Me

by Cynthia L. Hallen

*W*hen I was a child playing make-believe, I named my dolls and my imaginary friends "Catherine with a C," and "Joanna" and "Christina."

I knew nothing of my forebearers then. But now I know that these were the beautiful names of my foremothers. My ancestors must have been near me even when I was a little girl at play.

Later, when I joined the Church, studied linguistics, and began to teach at Brigham Young University, a number of doors were opened to me that inspired me to search for my ancestors. As early as 1976, my ninety-one-year-old Great-aunt Elizabeth had told me that her father, Godfrey (in German, Gottfried) Hallen, had immigrated from Dusseldorf, Germany. But without the name of a specific parish or hometown, I had never been able to trace the Hallen family beyond their arrival in Wisconsin and their lives in a home that was no longer standing.

Finally, in the years 2000 and 2001, I had several dreams about this pioneer home of the Hallen family in Marinette, Wisconsin. In my dreams, I distinctly felt the presence of some of my forebearers telling me a specific message: important material was now available to me in the second story of the house. When I ascended the stairwell in my dreams, I found that the rooms were filled with shelves of clothing, fabric, accessories, and other personal treasures.

The door opened to the most valued treasures of my life in an unexpected way. In June of 2001, I received a phone call from Susan Anneveldt, a genealogist who had studied linguistics under me at Brigham Young University in order to pursue a career in family history. Susan informed me that she had made an important discovery. On a brand new CD of emigration records from Dusseldorf, Germany, she had found my great-grandfather's name!

Great-grandfather Gottfried Hallen, who lived in Spellen, Germany, with his parents and several siblings, had applied for passage to the United States in February of 1856!

Because Susan had located the microfilm for Spellen in the Salt Lake Family History Library, I was able to begin extracting the names of my father's forebearers. As I recorded the names of my female ancestors, I noticed that many of them corresponded with the names I had used for my playmates in childhood. Now they were with me again. As I spent all of my spare time extracting the family names, I felt the spirits of my Hallen line with me constantly. They hovered in my thoughts, my dreams, and my sleep. They worked with me and walked with me.

Many other doors began to open for me since the day my student found my great-grandfather's name. But one of my most rewarding experiences happened when, as a linguistics teacher at BYU, I was presented with the opportunity to attend a professional linguistics conference in Norway in the summer of 2001. This was a doorway I had not expected. I was thrilled.

With anticipation, I urged my mother to come with me. "We'll go to Sweden while we're in Europe, and we'll visit some of your father's people." My grandfather Ture Viktor Forsstrom, born in 1901, exactly a hundred years before, had emigrated to America from the parish of Ljustorp, near Sundsvall, in 1925. Before the journey, I worked diligently to augment and copy family history records to present as a gift to our cousins, and as a memorial to our ancestors in Sweden. A professional genealogist told me that Sweden has the best family history records in the world.

It was true. I found invaluable treasures as I opened the door to a Sundsvall apartment where we met Sven Forsstrom and his sister Mary, my grandfather's first cousins. I told them we had come to visit the Ljustorp birthplace of our grandfather and to give some of the family members my gift of this history.

Mary and Sven graciously offered to take us to the parish of Ljustorp. Then, when I showed them the family history papers, Cousin Mary looked at me with light in her eyes. "I have a granddaughter who started doing this kind of work," she told me in Swedish. "And she speaks English!" I was stunned! I had a Swedish cousin who had begun to research her genealogy. Soon Mary was on the phone calling her granddaughter Gabriella Bylund on the island of Alno. She arranged for us to visit Gabriella after our trip to Ljustorp.

The visit to my grandfather's birthplace in Ljustorp was one of the most inspirational experiences I have ever had. It was beautiful. We arrived at about 4 P.M. Fields of emerald grass were waving in the wind, like waves of the ocean. The spirits of my ancestors seemed to move forward to welcome me, as if accepting the offering I had prepared for them in the Lord's temples and in my book of remembrance. As the clouds moved above us, patches of golden light and blue shadow would highlight the green landscape with unspeakable beauty. On the road ahead of us stood the pure white Lutheran church of Ljustorp. A brilliant golden sun-disk was the keystone for the doorway into the church, and another sun-disk ornamented the gate into the cemetery terraces below the church.

The genealogist that I had hired speculated that the word "Ljustorp" might mean "onion farm." But a pocket dictionary explained that "ljus" means "light" and "torp" means "croft," or "settlement." Ljustorp is aptly named the "croft of light." I was reminded of one of my favorite scriptures from Isaiah:

> Then shall thy light break forth as the morning, and thine health shall spring forth speedily: and thy righteousness shall go before thee; the glory of the Lord shall be thy rereward. . . . And if thou draw out thy soul to the hungry, and satisfy the afflicted soul; then shall thy light rise in obscurity, and thy darkness be as the noonday: And the Lord shall guide thee continually, and satisfy thy soul in drought, and make

fat thy bones: and thou shalt be like a watered garden, and like a spring of water, whose waters fail not. (Isaiah 58:8, 10-11)

In the graveyard, Mary used a green water pitcher provided at the cemetery spigot to wash the gravestones and refresh the flowers growing for each deceased family member. As we approached the church, Sven told us that we might not be able to enter because these days the churches were always locked to prevent vandalism.

Suddenly a groundskeeper drove his truck into the parking lot. Graciously, the worker unlocked the chapel for us before he drove away. We were able to enter the sanctuary where our ancestors had worshiped the Lord for hundreds of years. In the foyer of the church I found a metal plaque with a sacred inscription in Swedish which I later translated:

> LJUSTORP I JULI
> Thou who treadest herein,
> Do not forget that this is
> A holy place and
> A portal to heaven.
> Be silent and still
> With respect for this sacred room,
> And with mindfulness for those
> Who here celebrated the Sacrament.
> Pray to God, thy Father in Heaven,
> In spirit and truth.
> Listen with reverence to the word
> Of Jesus Christ, thy Savior.
> Become a living stone,
> The temple of the Spirit,
> God's church and gathering.
> God bless thy coming in and going out
> From now and till eternity.

Those words seemed like a message directly to me from my

ancestors, like a long-awaited patriarchal blessing.

After we left Ljustorp, we were then able to walk through the door of the home of Mary's granddaughter Gabriella on Alno Island. As we entered I could sense a lot of activity in the background. I discovered that Gabriella was printing out twenty-six pages of pedigree charts and family group sheets for me! She had traced one line back to A.D. 1200 for an ancestor named Fale Bure, who had helped deliver the king from his enemies. With the help of a computer and the Internet, Gabriella had been doing family history research for just one year. If I had traveled to Sweden the summer before, she would not have been able to share any family history records with me. We became friends instantly, and Gabriella welcomed me to return to her home so that we could do more research together.

After I returned to Utah, I worked for a year to process the new data and document the information with microfilm copies from the Salt Lake Family History Library and the Grove Creek Stake Family History Center. But this windfall had not meant that my doors had closed. In 2002, Gabriella sent me a letter urging me to come to Sweden again.

And though it was expensive, I decided to make airline reservations to fly at the end of August.

A week before I left, by happenstance, I met the former student of mine, Susan Anneveldt, who had found my Grandfather Hallen's name for me. She happened to find me as I was copying Swedish microfilms in the Salt Lake Family History Library. She brought me a brochure to sign up for a seminar at the library, sponsored by the Federation of Swedish Genealogical Societies. Participants were able to register as a member of the DISBYT computerized family history cooperative. We also submitted research questions to the Swedish experts in the seminar who would respond to us later by e-mail.

During my successful week in Sweden, Gabriella and her family graciously took me into their home and we photographed Ljustorp, tape-recorded the cousins in a mini-reunion, and worked on genealogy together. As we tried to use my new

DISBYT password to find some of Gabriella's maternal relatives, we had problems. But Gabriella found an unexpected solution when she went to the "ROTAR" (Roots) website.

Annika Lindquist, also of Alno, had responded to one of my research queries because she was distantly related to us in the Forsstrom line.

When Gabriella and I arrived at the home of Annika and her husband, Lennart, they were able to extract my data from a floppy disk and send it to the DISBYT administrators, who promptly gave me a new password for more effective research.

In addition, Annika and Lennart provided us with a soft-bound copy of a book containing the names and dates of all of our relatives and their neighbors in the parish of Ljustorp from the years 1500 to 1800. I came home from Sweden literally carrying another harvest of family history on my shoulders! Not only have I been able to extract the names of direct-line and collateral ancestors in my grandfather's hometown for temple ordinances, but I have also been able to use the book as a database for linguistic research on Swedish naming patterns.

My poem, "Ancestral Onomastics," expresses some of the feelings I had when I had been blessed to bring back so much information from my second trip to Ljustorp:

> In Sweden's croft of light, behold,
> Names and lives of predecessors.
> Back to Pleasant Grove with records,
> Sons and daughters on my shoulder.
> As I sheave the harvest, listen.
> My home fills with angel orders.
> Breath and line of household courses,
> Ljustorp's cradle holds our christening.

The cradle mentioned in the last line has special meaning, for during a third trip to Sweden in the summer of 2004, my relatives told me that my grandfather's "cradle" was on display upstairs in the homestead museum in Ljustorp. We were able to visit the museum and take photographs of the birch-basket cradle that had nestled many children in my grandfather's family.

I was also able to combine my family history research with my work as a linguistics professor at Brigham Young University. In August 2004, on the way to Sweden, I presented a paper at a historical linguistics conference in Copenhagen, on Swedish naming patterns. If nothing else, these naming patterns show how important lineage has always been to the Swedish people.

In the patronymic system of Scandinavian people, children often receive the first names of their grandparents and parents in addition to using the first name of their father as a surname. In Swedish records, the names of the children often turn to the parents, and the names of the parents turn to the children. This gives us specific clues for identifying ancestors whose names are missing in our records.

About 75 percent of all individuals in Ljustorp had shared just eight different male and eight different female given names for the past three hundred years. This duplication of first names across generations comes from the Western European practice of naming children after grandparents, parents, aunts, and uncles. For example, 89.72 percent of parents in Ljustorp named their first son after the father's father, the mother's father, the father, or an uncle. Furthermore, 67.77 percent named their first daughter after the father's mother, the mother, or an aunt. The pattern also holds for subsequent children born into the family. Knowing this pattern can help people with their family history research because the names of the children give clues about the parents, and the names of the parents give clues about the children.

I know that the doors of both heaven and earth have been opened to me.

The joy of associating with my ancestors through research has abundantly blessed my life. My hope is that every researcher will find this joy as their ancestors reach out to them from beyond the veil.

Making the Work Complete

by Ruth Martinson

I don't believe it was just a coincidence that early in my marriage, we spent a year living with my parents. It was during this time that I got so much information that now almost fifty years later I am still doing the temple work for most of these relatives. I can't really put my finger on it, but so often I feel that I'm getting help from beyond the veil.

For example, my mother-in-law Pansy was baptized into the Church in Denver in 1942. Three years later, she went to Salt Lake City and received her endowment. She also did the temple work for her deceased husband, her father, two sisters, and two of her children. Her own mother was still living at the time, so Pansy could not do her work. This woman did not die until two years later, in 1947, so the work would have had to be completed after that.

However, Pansy never made it back to Salt Lake City, home to the only nearby temple at the time. Finally, in 1954, she passed away.

In 1956, we were living in Flint, Michigan. One night I had a strange dream that woke me up. Three people were standing by my bed, just looking at me. They didn't say a word, but I knew who they were. It was Pansy—my mother-in-law—and her parents. I had never known her parents, but I knew instantly who they were. I never forgot that dream.

When we moved from Louisiana to Utah in 1970, I went to the Family History Library every week for four years. When I checked the archives, I found the family group sheet that Pansy had submitted. I thought she had done her family's temple work. But when I looked at it, I could see that although she had done her mother's temple work, and had sealed her mother and father together, she herself was not sealed to her parents. She had probably done their work by mail.

At once I understood what the dream meant. She wanted to be sealed to her parents. With joy in my heart, still vividly remembering those three visitors at my bedside that night in my dream, I completed that work for them. They had come knowing that I would help them. And they would not have to come again.

In My Grandmother's Name

by Meg Vogl

*E*ver since I was sixteen, I have had a great love for family history work. Because I was the only member of the Church in my family, I have submitted many ancestors' names so that their temple ordinances might be performed.

After my maternal grandmother died in February of 1993, I eagerly awaited the end of the required year before submitting her name for ordinance work at the Chicago Illinois Temple. At the time, family names were held for a limited period in a family file at the temple until family members could perform the ordinance work.

When many months passed and still I had not been able to get to the temple, which was a seven-hour drive away in Chicago, I felt that my grandmother might be feeling anxious. So, reluctantly, I called the temple and asked that her name be moved to the temple file, where it would be given at random to members performing ordinance work. I had been close to my grandmother while she was alive—I was her namesake. I felt disappointed that I couldn't do this essential work for her. But I knew these ordinances were important to her progression, and I was glad that at least the work would get done.

Some time later, in October of 1996, my husband had a week-long seminar in Chicago. When I accompanied him on this trip, I found I had an entire week that I could spend in the temple. What a treat!

All week long, I did ordinance after ordinance. On the last day, when it was near the time we would be driving home, I checked my watch. My husband was to pick me up at 5:15 P.M. It was 3:00, so I felt I had enough time to do one last session.

When I was given the name of the person I would be doing the work for, my mouth dropped open in astonishment. A year and a half after submitting it, I had been given my grandmother's name! I would have the blessing of being her proxy after all.

Some might claim that this experience was simply a remarkable coincidence. It is my feeling, however, that in His love and mercy, the Lord managed things so that I might realize the desire of my heart—to do something of eternal worth for my beloved grandmother that she could not do for herself.

"In My Grandmother's Name," by Meg Vogl.
Copyright Intellectual Reserve, Inc.
First published in the *Ensign*, April 2002.

Go Back to the Beginning

by Mable Jensen

fter many years of family history research, I had been able to do quite a bit of temple ordinance work on my side and on my husband's side, but I had always lacked the marriage date of my great-grandparents John Pickett and Rosetta Stringer. They had emigrated by ship from England in 1855, and all I knew was that they had been married during that voyage. I felt the answer must be somewhere, but I never expected to find it the way I did.

I was captain of the Daughters of Utah Pioneers Elmhurst Camp in Oakland, California, and we met each month to study the pamphlet *Treasures of Pioneer History*. At four o'clock on the day of one of our meetings, the phone rang and the woman calling told me that she was ill and would not be able to make her presentation that night. Could I please fill in? It was up to me.

With little time to prepare, I began to study the pamphlet. The first part seemed to go into quite a bit of detail about a boat, so I skipped over that part and started further on. But I had a strong impression I should go back to the beginning. I turned back to the first part, but I was impatient, so I skipped over it again.

A second time I felt impressed to go back. I did, but again it seemed to be too much to cover for the time I had to prepare, so again I skipped ahead. A third time I felt the distinct impression that I should go back and read. So I did.

Soon my eyes fell upon the names of my great-grandparents. Stunned, I read the entry for 17 April 1855, which stated that the

Chimborazo had sailed from Liverpool, England, with 432 Latter-day Saints aboard. The text continued: "Three marriages were celebrated on board tonight: John Pickett and Rosetta Stringer, and David Rees and Martha Eynon were united by President E. Stephenson; and David Williams and Ann Walters by President Thomas Jeremy in the Welsh language."

What I had thought was a tedious account became a treasure to me. Now I knew for sure when my great-grandparents had been married and by whom. I also knew the name of the ship and its departure point. Such information was priceless to me in my desire to make my ancestors' records accurate.

This experience taught me the value of listening and obeying the promptings of the Holy Spirit. My life has been greatly enriched as I've recognized the Lord's concern for me and my ancestors.

"Go Back to the Beginning," by Mable Jensen.
Copyright Intellectual Reserve, Inc.
First published in the *Ensign*, April 1999.

A Visit in a Dream
by Janet Schurig

*W*hen I was trying to research the family structure of my ancestors in England, I had such an unusual dream that I awoke startled. I saw the image of a young girl who had been a household servant in an upper-middle-class household. She was very real to me. I saw this thirteen-year-old girl in her bed in her small, undecorated bedroom.

Though I didn't hear her speak—I'm not even sure she was aware of me at all—I knew what had happened to her. Dressed in a very plain shift with her red-gold hair streaming straight down her back, her expression was one of pain and despair. I felt her pain. She had been raped by her master, yet she was unable to leave the household where she served him.

Betrayed and abused, with her heart in despair, she was sick with grief. As I learned later, she bore two children of this master.

Then the dream shifted to a later time. I saw the girl now grown into a woman. She was beautiful and well dressed. Her red-blonde hair curled under a fashionable bonnet. She had been able to get away from the household, but had now returned to visit one of the children. At the time, I was not sure what the dream meant.

Years later I was fortunate enough to be able to afford the services of a very wonderful professional research assistant. Through her work on my extended ancestors, she found the records of a very large family. She began to go through the dates carefully. One day she called me with a serious problem. She had discovered there were four children whose birth dates were problematic. The two oldest children were born only a couple of months apart. The two youngest children were born only four or five months apart.

"This cannot be," my assistant said. "One mother would be unable to give birth this way. There must be two mothers." Of course. And in that moment, I returned in my mind to the image of the girl with the streaming hair. I was inspired that she was the mother of two of these children. The master's wife would not have wanted either of her husband's illegitimate children, and so a generous and loving brother of the abusive master had taken them into his family and raised them as his own with their cousins. Though the little girl died at about two months of age, he raised the little boy to manhood, claiming him and endowing him with his family name.

Because I had felt the abused mother's sorrow in the dream, I knew she wanted her children to be sealed to her. We did not know if she had married and had other children, though my dream indicated that she had taken charge of her life and would have been blessed with other children. However, because of my dream, we did not seal the two extra little children into the family, but prayed that they would find their mother beyond the veil.

A Letter from Russia

by Doris Lyon, as told to Vicki Blum

*W*hen I was a little girl in Germany, my country became involved in the Second World War. My brother Ernst was taken out of school at age sixteen and forced to join Hitler's army. After two years, Ernst was permitted to come home, but he soon became lonely and dissatisfied because all his friends were still fighting in the army. He asked my parents for permission to rejoin the army, but they refused. He pleaded with them, and eventually they consented. The day he left was the last time they saw him alive.

A year after the war ended, a letter from Ernst came from a hospital in Russian territory. Ernst said he was not allowed to write, and so he was sending the letter through a friend. He indicated that he had caught a mild illness while being transported from a Russian prison camp, but he expected to arrive home in about two weeks.

Two weeks passed, but Ernst did not come home. My parents wrote to the address on the letter, but the letter came back marked undeliverable.

They wrote to every hospital, to the mayor of the city, and to anyone they thought could help them. Despite their coordinated efforts with the Red Cross over the course of thirty years, my parents never were able to find out what had happened to their son.

When I grew up, I immigrated to Canada and there joined The Church of Jesus Christ of Latter-day Saints. When it came time for me to go to the temple, I discovered that I could not have Ernst sealed to the rest of the family because I did not have proof of his death. I remembered the missionaries telling me to exercise faith in Heavenly Father and that He would help me through my difficulties. I knelt down and prayed mightily. I explained my problem—that I needed information about Ernst in order to have him sealed to the family. I asked Father in Heaven to send me proof of Ernst's death.

About eight weeks later, my brother Paul telephoned me. "Doris," he said, "the strangest thing has happened." Then he told me the following story.

A few weeks earlier, a document had been sent from the Russian Red Cross to the German Red Cross. The German Red Cross translated the document and sent it to the house where my parents had lived in Dormagen, West Germany. Since my parents had died many years earlier, the letter was returned to the German Red Cross, who promptly sent it back to my parents' home. The letter went back and forth two or three times until a postman who had known my family personally delivered it to my sister Hilda, who still lives in Germany. The letter told of Ernst's death on 28 September 1946.

I have a very strong testimony that Heavenly Father hears and answers prayers. He knows how to help all his children because, as he declared to Moses, "all things are numbered unto me, for they are mine and I know them" (Moses 1:35).

"A Letter from Russia,"
by Doris Lyon, as told to Vicki Blum.
Copyright Intellectual Reserve, Inc.
First published in the *Ensign*, January 1997.

Break Through into the Light

by Lincoln Fuqua

As a young man, I was privileged to receive one of the greatest blessings of my life: I found The Church of Jesus Christ of Latter-day Saints.

But it was several years later—after my marriage to my sweetheart Carol, after medical school, and after many of my miraculous business opportunities—that I finally understood one of the most amazing events of my childhood: a remarkable dream that had come to me when I was a small boy of ten.

I have never forgotten the vivid images of this dream. I saw myself trapped in a cavern of darkness with masses of people—and the strong feeling I had was that all of them were close to me, like family and friends. Of all those present, I was the first one to see the tiny ray of light emanating from a distant wall. At once the others offered their help to me, and with their assistance, I made my way there. Together, we dug open a hole big enough for me to fall forward into a brilliantly lit room. I called it a "star chamber of time."

The "star chamber" was a strange and marvelous phenomenon, like a huge urim and thummim. Inside the "star chamber of time" were massive collections of records—on tablets, in storage bins, stone jars, and in many other forms. It was impressed upon my young mind in this dream that these records were of a valuable historical nature—all about the lives of many civilizations. On the walls of the chamber were symbols that looked like those found in pyramids.

Some resembled Indian petroglyphs. In the center of the

65

floor was the room's sole source of light, a large stone altar or podium rising like a stalagmite, but with the sharp pointed top sheared off to create a flat table of stone. The light increased to a brighter intensity near the top of this "altar," glowing through the flat surface as through a giant quartz crystal. At its base, the color was the same as the gray marble-like texture of the room.

As I moved toward the flat-toped stone, I felt empowered by a force of some kind of light or energy that flowed down from my head to my feet. The curious stone had attracted my attention because it was as though it had an intelligence of its own. The feeling generated in me by the stone's aura engendered some kind of empowerment that came down over me such that I was able to see and feel what I remember perceiving as a vivid living record of history.

All of a sudden it was as though I were personally integrated into the events before me in time. This force allowed me to engage the stone "table of time," to put into motion the viewing of a giant collection of data and media resources and records concerning the past, and even the future events in my own life as a missionary, mission president, physician, educator, fund-raiser, and developer.

Though my conversion to the Church took place many years after this dream I had as a ten-year-old boy, my life became much clearer to me in relationship to what had happened that night. And the key—the opening to the star chamber of time—was a miracle that took place as I began to search for my relatives. Though I had begun to dabble in some genealogical research, I had found the same barriers that many people find—puzzling records, names that had no connections or seemed lost with alternate spellings.

The miracle was a visit from a woman who helped me to widen the entry into the most wonderful spectacle of light I could possibly have asked for. One night, she came into my room and stood by my bed. She had an important message for me. She was from my family, she told me, an ancestor from colonial Maryland. Her name was Mary Hatch, the sister-in-law of colonial Maryland Governor Josias Fendall, who served from 1656-1660.

Her identity had been confused with that of her more famous sister, also named Mary, who had married the governor. In my mind's eye, she showed me where her records were. She promised me if I would look in this record, I would be blessed to find many other precious records of my noble ancestry. It would open up to me a vast archive of material from the past. And she said I must do the temple work for thousands of people who were waiting for me.

The next morning, I went to the Salt Lake Genealogical Library, and in the Maryland stacks of printed family histories, I saw the little blue book that she had shown me the night before. I was third in line to reach the material, and as I gazed at the shelves ahead of me, I saw a blue book pulled out a little on the shelf, easy to spot. Yes, that was the book I was looking for, already slightly pulled out so that I could see it. I instantly turned to page 83 in the Bean Family History of Maryland, and sure enough, there on that very page she had shown me was her record. In that very spot, I found the names I needed, which opened up to me the discovery that I was the literal descendant of many of the nation's founding fathers and other colonial families that helped to lay the foundation of our great nation before our family migrated to Kentucky after the Revolution. I was then led to many additional records, as she promised, wherein I discovered the connecting lines through which my wife and I were related.

Over the years we discovered our connection to some ninety governors of twenty-one states and nearly three hundred U.S. Senators, Congressmen, and Supreme Court justices. Our hearts leaped for joy when we also found that General George Washington and his wife's first cousin's husband, the prophet of the American Revolution, Patrick Henry, were numbered among our tenth-generation ancestors. Patrick Henry had served as the Speaker of the Virginia House of Burgesses where nineteen other members of our family tree had served. He was the first governor of the Commonwealth of Virginia and served five terms. He later purchased the Fuqua family "Red Hill" plantation when he moved to Kentucky to claim his land grant. Our Fuqua Family

Foundation has helped to support the work of the boys' home that still exists on the estate near Appomattox, Virginia, where Patrick Henry is also interred.

In our lines we also discovered Daniel Boone, Colonel James Bowie of the Alamo, Abraham Lincoln, Jefferson Davis, Robert E. Lee, and Ulysses S. Grant. Their friendships during that period led to the future intermarriages that allowed us to be numbered among their honored descendants.

During further research we were able to tie our family's lineage to thirty-one of the forty-one presidents of the United States, and further link our family's heritage to the royal families of Europe. We discovered that our thirty-third generation great-grandfather, Sahier de Quincey, was the author of the Magna Carta of 1215. We were further amazed to find that the families of twenty-six of the signers, along with King John, had all inter-married into our lines. Their great-grandfather was King Henry I of France. This lineage enabled us to further trace our family's heritage directly to the ancient prophets Abraham, Isaac, and Jacob of the House of Israel, and on back to the ancient patriarch Adam. We have created a family tree scroll that shows the direct lineage of this holy royal priesthood family through the many generations from my grandson through the lineage of King James and Joseph of Arimathea (the Great).

Due to more divinely inspired research, we discovered the records of our eleventh-generation ancestor Count Nicolas Fou-quet, who was the Attorney General for the French Parliament, and the Minister of Finance for Louis XVI, the Sun King. He helped to build the exquisite Vaux Le Vicomte Chateau, the larg-est chateau in all of France at the time. It was larger and grander in beauty than the King's Palace, the Fontainebleau. His godfa-ther was the Cardinal of France, who was also his father's business partner. Nicolas's father, Francois Fouquet, and four earlier gen-erations of grandfathers named Francois back to 1510 held seats in the French Parliament. On Easter weekend of 1998, Carol and I witnessed the moment when our Great-uncle Nicolas and his wife received their endowment blessings of the Lord's Kingdom, and we felt the power of those blessings as they affected many others of that era.

Genealogy became one of our crowning passions. With energy and joy we contributed financially and intellectually to the improvements of the genealogy libraries of the Church. Of all of the achievements of our lives, the sacred redeeming work we have been able to perform for those thousands of our beloved, noble, kindred ancestors in the house of the Lord will undoubtedly be the most precious legacy we shall leave to succeeding generations of our posterity. My childhood dream of the masses of people in the darkness came true. I was blessed to have broken through the wall.

They Are Waiting

by Velma Skidmore

As far back as I can remember, my mother and father did family history research. After they died—within two weeks of each other in 1975—my older sister sent me a part of their family records on our Bradford ancestors. I placed them in my basement storeroom in the box in which they came. And there the information sat for at least fifteen years—undisturbed.

At least it was undisturbed until my daughter's youth group planned a temple trip to do baptisms. Our bishop had suggested that the youth bring names of their ancestors. Then I remembered the box in the basement. As I climbed the stairs with it, I thought how active my parents had been in family history research, and I was hoping that there might be some information about someone we could process so that my daughter might be able to perform a baptism for them in the temple.

The box contained two fat notebooks, neatly organized, with family group sheets accompanied by photographs, newspaper clippings, and source notes. I knew that my parents had not been able to continue their work on family history during the last ten years of their lives due to mission service and deteriorating health, which meant that a quarter of a century had passed since anything was done with these particular records.

Reflecting on this, I remembered that my mother had been given two patriarchal blessings—one when she was ten years old, and then for some reason another one when she was an adult. Both blessings mentioned that she would be responsible for her family's history. And I thought, *My mother has had this responsibility since she was ten years old! No wonder she spent so much time at it.* I reread her blessings. One of them specifically says, "Many of thine ancestors are waiting anxiously in the spirit world for thee to liberate them through thy work in the temple."

That hit me hard. I remembered the many times my mother asked me for assistance to help her type information she found because I could type and she couldn't. Sadly I remembered that I did it reluctantly. Thinking about it has often brought tears to my eyes. Now, with these two notebooks, I thought I might be able to carry on some of her work that had never been finished.

I could also see that my parents' research had been accomplished without the use of photocopying machines and computers. Although they went to the temple as often as they could, they lived over four hundred miles from the nearest one. In fact, I remember while growing up that I thought my mother was obsessed with the mailbox. She would hurry to it whenever the mail was delivered. Now I realize it was because she was looking for answers to her inquiries.

As my daughter and I began to thumb through the records to find a name whose work had not been done—as we began to check the records—we were amazed. Name after name had no record of having their work done. We were stunned. We checked all of the material, and no, none of these names had been baptized or received their ordinances!

We stopped looking after a hundred and three names. We both thought that was enough for now. My daughter would be happy to perform baptisms for as many as she could. But we could see that she might have to enlist help.

The day the young people performed the baptisms was a good day. As the baptisms were taking place, the temple president came into the baptismal font area. It seemed he wanted to talk to one of the youth leaders. He was carrying some documents. He asked the leader, "Who is the Skidmore?" Someone close by pointed out my daughter to him. He looked at her and acknowledged her with a small nod. "Her ancestors have been anxiously waiting for this work to be done," he said.

Never, never before have I had such strong spiritual feelings. Even today as I write this, or whenever I look through the two notebooks or talk about it—as I was once asked to do in stake conference—I get that same strong spiritual feeling.

As I began to prepare the names from the two notebooks to send to Salt Lake City for clearance, I wondered how I would ever send in that many names. So I decided to photocopy all the family group sheets and send them that way.

When my work arrived in Salt Lake City I received a phone call saying, "We received all of these family group sheets on forms the Church hasn't used for at least thirty years." I explained why they were sent that way. I was anxious, feeling that they might not be accepted. But the woman on the phone was understanding. "Well, now we understand," she said. And the names were cleared.

With help from many others in the days that followed, temple ordinances were completed for six hundred and fifty-three ancestors whose names were found between the covers of the two old notebooks.

The Greatest Sacrifice

by Benjamin Nelson

*L*ord Soma's family genealogy, called the *Chi Ken Marokashi*, was acclaimed as the best in Japan.

Lord Soma was a wealthy man with a vast estate. He had many servants to do his work, and samurai warriors to protect him.

One night, his mansion caught fire and began to burn with intensity. Everyone fled outside to safety. They watched with horror as the building began to crumble to the ground.

As Lord Soma watched the fire, he said: "I feel no regret about the house and all its furnishings, even if they burn to the very last piece, because they are things that can be replaced later on. I only regret that I was unable to take out the genealogy, which is my family's most precious treasure."

It was at this moment that one of the samurai among those attending him, called out, "I will go in and take it out."

Lord Soma and the others laughed and said, "The house is already engulfed in flames. How are you going to take it out?"

Now, this samurai had never been very good with words, and he knew he had never been useful as a warrior, but being a man who always finished what he started, he had been valued as an attendant. He said to the people who were watching the fire: "I have never been of use to my master because I am so careless. But I have resolved that someday my life should be of use to him. This seems to be that time."

Without saying another word, the samurai who loved Lord Soma turned and ran into the flames.

Shocked, the group backed away, their arms in front of their faces to hide their looks of fear and to protect themselves from the heat. It seemed impossible that the samurai could come out of the flames with the genealogy. They were stunned.

Finally, after the fury of the fire died down, they kept watching to see if the samurai would return. But there was no movement, nothing.

The next day, after the flames had been extinguished, some of the servants and other samurai began to sift around in the ashes for anything that might remain. They were still puzzled as to how this man could have run into the fire while they stood, dumbfounded, watching him disappear.

Lord Soma shook his head in sorrow. "Look for his remains. What a pity he had to die."

Looking everywhere, Lord Soma and his servants combed through the ashes for several hours before they came to the garden adjacent to the living quarters. There, against the soil, lying like a hump on the earth was a charred, unrecognizable corpse.

Carefully, they turned over the badly blackened body. It was the samurai, all right. But they noticed something unusual. There was blood flowing against the ground. A long slash had been made in the center of his body. And as they looked, they saw something else. Stunned, they pulled the corpse to a larger space against the garden wall. There was something inside the samurai's body that he had placed there. It was the genealogy!

Amazed, Lord Soma stood with tears in his eyes. The brave samurai had protected the sacred genealogy with his life.

Retold from *Hagakure: The Book of the Samurai*, by Yamamoto Tsunetomo, translated by Scott Wilson. Tokyo: Kodansha International, 2000.

A Cry for Help

by Don Millgate

*T*hough we moved our home from Orem to Fountain Green, Utah, I was still working in Provo as a training supervisor for Deseret Industries. The move meant a longer commute for me, but we were excited about living in this historic area, where many pioneer forefathers had carved a rich legacy.

In our drives along the commute, we saw from the road a couple of monuments built to commemorate these brave pioneers. One of these monuments, we later discovered, honored a pioneer family and two farm workers who had been massacred by renegade Indians at Uintah Springs, or Salt Creek. After their bishop asked them to move from Santaquin to Mount Pleasant, they buried their guns so they would not be tempted to promote violence. Unprotected, they had a picnic lunch by Salt Creek, where they were brutally killed. Legends had been told that there had been a child with them, but there was no proof.

We moved into our Fountain Green home on Thanksgiving weekend. It was that Monday, as I began the long drive down Salt Creek Canyon to go to work in Provo, that I passed one of the monuments and thought I heard someone talking to me. It was a woman's voice—quiet, loving, but commanding. "Don, Don, Don, please get our temple work done."

The voice was so strong and clear that I automatically turned my head to see who had spoken. I even turned to look in the back seat of my automobile, but there wasn't anyone there. I slowed down as I drove down the canyon, my mind racing with questions. When I got to the road that turns right and goes up over the Mt. Nebo Loop, I pulled over.

I was quite shaken and said to myself, "Did I really hear what I thought I heard?" I don't have a radio in the car, so it wasn't that. I work with mentally and physically handicapped people, and I have seen what happens when schizophrenic patients haven't taken their medication. Was I becoming schizophrenic too?

Although only one woman seemed to be speaking to me, I had a sense that there were five others in this group also.

I sat, stunned, thinking about what seemed to be occurring. I said to my Heavenly Father, "Is this really happening to me?"

A peaceful, reassuring feeling came over me, calming me until finally my thoughts turned to the fact that I might be late for work. So I drove on to Provo.

After work, as I drove back home and passed the monument again, I heard that same sweet voice say, "Don, please, *please* get our temple work done." I couldn't deny that I had heard her message this time. And along with her plea, this time I could hear a baby crying.

The next morning, I mentioned my experience to my wife, Shirley. We discussed the possibility that even though a monument had been erected to commemorate these people, it seemed that no one had done their temple work. How could they have been forgotten?

The following Sunday when I mentioned my experience to the members in our high priest meeting, they discussed what had happened, and said they thought I might be talking about the massacre at Uintah Springs. Brother Ballard of our ward said that on his way to work he always drove by the Pioneer Chronological Library. He told me he could get some help to research the names. He suggested I go down to the monument and copy the names off the plaque.

So, after Church, I drove down to the monument, where again I heard the same sweet voice asking that their work be done. I copied the names: Jens Jorgensen and his wife, Christian E. Kjeruli, and a second man, Jens Terkelsen. When I gave these names to Brother Ballard, he took the information to a researcher, who told him he would look up the information.

For the next several months I waited, still hearing this woman's cry every time I passed the monument. I finally had to plead with her, "Please, I haven't heard anything yet. You'll have to be patient a little while longer."

Then one Saturday, May 13, 1994, Brother Ballard came by to see me. My wife and I were working in the yard. Brother Ballard had a knowing look on his face and a twinkle in his eye. He handed me a large manila envelope, saying as he did, "The researcher said to give this to Brother Millgate. He's the one who received the message. He's the one who was spiritually in tune to hear and receive it. He should be the one to do the work for these people."

Inside the envelope was a temple-ready disk to be taken to the Manti Temple. Also in the envelope was a copy of the notice from the newspaper in 1858, which mentioned the deaths of three men and one woman. The article gave the name of the men and the one woman.

My jaw dropped open and I was speechless. I felt so humbled and amazed at the same time. Why me? I felt completely unworthy, yet honored to be able to do this temple work.

Later, my wife and I discussed who might help us do this work. We felt that our son and son-in-law would like the privilege of doing the work for the other two men. My wife and I would be proxy for Jens Jorgensen and his wife. We waited for our family members, but when they couldn't get their schedules together, my wife and I decided to go ahead and do the work as quickly as possible, as there had already been a delay of two or three weeks.

My wife had taken the temple-ready disk to the Manti Temple the Thursday after we'd received it. We went to the Manti Temple to do a session and discussed with the people at the desk that we wished them to do the baptism and ordinance work for us and that we would be there the following Saturday, June 10, 1994, to do the endowments and sealing for these people. Someone else could do the names of the other two men.

On Saturday we did the endowment work and sealing. After the sealing, while my wife was talking to another friend for a moment, I went around to the foot of the west spiral staircase. As I stood there, I felt the woman's presence. In that same sweet voice I had heard many times on my drive to Provo, she said, "Thank you, dear brother in the gospel."

After the sealing, as we were leaving, the greeter at the front desk stopped us and asked, "Are you the Millgates?" He told us that he was Gail Yorgason, and introduced us to his wife, Lucy. They were interested in what had taken place today because their son Blaine Yorgason had written about the Salt Creek Massacre.

As I talked to Gail, my wife stepped aside and visited with Lucy. Lucy told her that after Blaine's book had been published, they received a phone call from a woman who lives in northern Utah. She told the Yorgasons that she was the great-granddaughter of a little baby that had been found alive clinging to Mrs. Jorgensen's body. The baby had not been harmed.

I was shocked. We hadn't known about the baby. We hadn't read the book, *Massacre at Salt Creek* by Blaine Yorgason, or had any knowledge of it. No reference was made in any of the records or newspaper articles of the time. The thing that stunned me was that during the entire time we researched this incident, I had always mentioned "the group of five people." My wife had constantly reminded me that there were only three names on the monument, and that the newspaper had mentioned only one more.

I told my wife that on the second time I had passed that monument, I had heard the baby cry. The Indians had not wanted the little girl child, so they had left her unharmed. She was the fifth member of the group.

A Note in the Margin

by Monta B. Salmon

I did a lot of genealogy when my first two children were young, but as time went on and the demands of a growing family increased, I found I hadn't done any for some time. We had moved to a different town and had built a house. We lived in a different ward and stake, and my four siblings, who were living with us, had grown up and left home. I had three more babies, along with the usual school, community, and church responsibilities.

One day a close friend commented that they had just purchased a new computer and they were having the Personal Ancestral File (PAF) software installed on it. I knew a little about computers, but not much. It was obvious that the PAF she was speaking of was a genealogy program, but I didn't know anything about it. This was back in the days when home computers were fairly new. I had a computer at home. It was time I learned. So off I went to find this stake's Family History Center. I learned quickly that computer genealogy was great! Soon I was called to the staff of the Family History Center. My sister, who had meanwhile taken over the family research, asked me which line I wanted to work on. I remembered seeing an Angus McLeod and his family on a Canadian census many years earlier, and I knew that for some reason not much had been done on this line. So I chose to work on this Scottish McLeod line.

There was not a lot of information about this line. My sister gave me all she had on our McLeods. They had come to Canada in the 1830s. We knew that there were three brothers who came, including our ancestor Angus and his two brothers, Peter and Donald. We knew that Peter had never married and was fairly well-off, owning at least two different farms. We knew that Donald had married but had no children. We also knew that Angus had married Sarah McGill in Scotland and had left for Canada with two small children, William and John. According to family legend, little John had died during the voyage. More children were born in Canada.

We were encouraged when my sister found a document in land records that told us a great deal about the McLeod family. The landowner, Peter McLeod, left one of his farms to a son of Angus. The other farm was left to their brother Donald and his wife, Catherine Keith. They were to live on it during their lifetime. When they died it was to be passed on to his two sisters, Margaret McLeod and Nancy McLeod, who both lived in Scotland.

Peter died in 1852. Donald and his wife lived on the farm for several years. Donald died about 1864. However, Catherine didn't die until 1896. She had remarried a man by the name of William Rose. At her death, the relatives of her second husband were interested in buying the land. By this time, the sister heirs, Margaret and Nancy, had died in Scotland. A "quit claim" deed was drawn up. The descendants of Margaret and Nancy, still in Scotland, signed this document, saying that they had no interest in the land.

The land records gave me wonderful information. I now had a list that named the descendants of both Margaret and Nancy, along with their locations in Scotland in 1900. So I went to work trying to figure out how they all fit together. It took some time. I went through fifty years of birth, marriage, and death indexes, and paid for certificates from Scotland. Bit by bit, I followed them back until I got to the time period when registrations were filmed. Then I ordered film after film, following the families and putting them together.

At last the time came that I felt my work would provide a connection. I knew that on this day I was going to read the film that would name the parents of the family I was building. The mother had to be either Margaret or Nancy McLeod. That name would eventually lead me to her parents. I was so excited; I couldn't wait to get to the Family History Center. There was no doubt in my mind that today was the day.

Knowing that they were from the island of Islay in Western Scotland, I had often complained to my genealogy buddies, "If these people wanted me to find them so badly, why didn't they write their names somewhere?" I knew these ancestors wanted me to find them. And I was determined I was going to be successful on this particular day.

I pulled the film out, put it on the reader, and turned to the correct birth registration. There it was. Now, I thought, the next thing I'll see is the mother's name.

But whoops—the name on the film was Margaret McCuaig, not Margaret McLeod. I was puzzled. Where had I gone wrong? I rechecked everything. I reevaluated my decisions. But I couldn't find any mistake. I was at a standstill.

I decided to go back and go through everything again, making sure I was doing it right. I would continue to build the families. Perhaps something would make itself clear to me or perhaps I just needed to go back one more generation. I would just keep plugging away at it.

A month or so later I was looking at a birth registration. There are three on a page, and the one I wanted was the middle one of the three. Both the one I was looking at and the one above had the surname "McCuaig." Suddenly I noticed a note in the margin, probably written by the registrar. It said, "McLeod and McCuaig are the same name. The family signs both ways." What? Could it be? McLeod and McCuaig are nothing alike. How could they possibly be the same name?

A week or so later my sister came for a visit, so I took her over to the Family History Center, telling her I had something I wanted her to look at. But I didn't tell her anything about what it was. I showed her the note in the margin. She stared at it without moving for about thirty seconds. Then, being more brilliant than

I am, she quickly turned and ran for the computers. She typed Angus McCuaig into the International Genealogical Index (IGI) on Family Search and it came up with a marriage to Sarah McGill and the birth of two sons, William and John. These were the people I was looking for! Everything fit! The Margaret McCuaig I had found earlier was indeed our Margaret McLeod.

Since then, our genealogy on the McLeod/McCuaig line has blossomed. The Island of Islay is quite literally covered with McCuaigs. In fact, the name I had complained had not been written anywhere is written everywhere. We have had the privilege of sending hundreds of names to the temple. We have learned that it was not uncommon for the McLeods and McCuaigs to switch back and forth between names, and even more common for them to use the McLeod name exclusively when they immigrated to other countries.

I have been overwhelmed to think that 150 years ago, a loving Heavenly Father inspired a humble clerk in a small, rural registration office to write those few words of explanation in the margin so that I might understand and connect my McLeod/McCuaig family. That clerk's act was probably of little consequence to him, but to our family it meant the difference of hundreds and hundreds of our ancestors whose names we have found and continue to gather.

A Family Lost and Found

by Pat L. Sagers

*L*ucile Embley met Robert Leo Sagers at a dance at the Terrace Ballroom in Salt Lake City. It seemed to be love at first sight for them both.

Though Lucile had plans to move to California with some friends to work for a while, she continued corresponding with Leo. It wasn't long before she followed her heart, accepted his marriage proposal, came back to Salt Lake City, and married him.

Leo loved the outdoors, especially hunting and camping. He and Lucile had many good times together. But he had one fault that became hard to overlook—a drinking problem. When Leo wasn't drinking, he was a lot of fun and everyone loved to be around him. But when he drank, he became a different person.

In order for Lucile to feel comfortable with Leo, she also began drinking. Soon most of their entertainment was in beer joints and lounges. This wasn't the kind of lifestyle that Lucile wanted. But drinking had become a necessity for Leo. It seemed he couldn't stop—not even when they began having children. They were working at it with the birth of the first son, Gary. But when little Lynn was born, Lucile had finally had enough. When Lynn was three months old, she made the decision to divorce Leo.

After the divorce, Leo left the area completely, never seeing his family again. He severed all ties—never even supporting or visiting his two sons in any way.

Alone during a time of war, Lucile found life became very

difficult for her. She felt the challenge keenly when little Gary came down with pneumonia. As the sole source of support for her children, she was forced to board out her two little boys during the week while she worked two different jobs. She worked from nine o'clock in the morning until two o'clock the next morning. But she refused to work on Saturday nights and Sundays—the only time she could bring her boys home with her to spend some time with them. This was a demanding life for Lucile, but she was able to get herself out of debt and support her children.

However, sometimes the most tragic circumstances repeat themselves. And they did for Lucile. She eventually became attracted to another alcoholic, Andrew Miller. And because she had been so lonely, she married him. Another son was born of this union—Louis. But this husband was even worse than Leo. He deceived Lucile, lying and cheating on her. Plus, he expected her to support him. It wasn't long before there was another divorce, and Andrew Miller moved out of the state also.

Twice was enough! Lucile did not remarry after that. She decided to advance herself by taking college classes while she continued to work hard to support her three sons and herself. Life was hard for Lucile, but she set high goals. There was no contact with either husband until much later, when the two older boys were grown. At last they saw their father, Leo, just before he died in a nursing home. They attended his funeral.

After Lucile had raised her sons, she was able to retire, go on some cruises with a group of friends, and serve as both Relief Society president and a stake missionary. She was also a temple ordinance worker in the Salt Lake Temple for many years until her health became so bad that she could no longer work there.

I, Pat Sagers, married Lucile's son Lynn. I had always had a great love for genealogy work, and for putting families together eternally. It always bothered me that with all the faithful Church work, and all the temple work that Lucile had done, she could not be sealed to her sons, since she had never married again. One day, I asked my husband how he thought his mother would feel if, after she died, we had her sealed to his father, Leo. Lynn immediately said, "Ooohh no! She would not like that." Lynn's brother Gary had never been allowed to use his middle name "Leo" because of his father. He had been instructed to use the initial "L." Lucile wanted nothing to do with Leo, and nothing to remind her of him, either.

As she grew older, Lucile had several heart attacks and bypass surgeries. Her health began to decline in her late seventies. Quite ill for the last couple of years of her life, she had been hospitalized with pneumonia several times. During one of these hospitalizations, she felt that she faced the most serious trial of her faith. In fact, she told Lynn and me that she had actually prayed to die. Realizing that she was being selfish, she had added a postscript to her prayer by saying, "But, Lord, not my will, but thine be done."

Lucile went on to live for a year or two after that. Her work was still unfinished. And because she lived longer, it was during this last time that she was able to receive some important inspiration—both for herself and for her family.

She woke up one night with a thought so strong in her mind that she couldn't return to sleep. She was impressed that she, Lucile, was the missing link that might bring her family into an eternal union.

The thought came so powerfully to her, and with such clarity, that she actually sat up in her bed and defensively asked out loud, "Why am I the missing link?"

After that incident, she kept getting promptings that she should go to the temple and be sealed to her first husband, Leo, who had died years before—the man who had given up his family for his addiction to alcohol. She began to understand that this was the only way that all of her boys could be sealed to her as a family throughout the eternities. She had always been aware that this was an earthly ordinance that she could have performed for herself, her sons, and for Leo too. But she knew that her heart had never let her proceed. It seemed more critical now. After she received this light and knowledge, she knew that this was a decision that she alone had to make. She also told them that she felt that her father, who had once been a bishop, had something to do with these promptings—that her father was probably working with Leo on the other side, helping him to become prepared.

Lucile asked her boys how they felt about being sealed to a father that they had seen only a couple of times in their adult lives—a man who had abandoned them, who had never really been a father to them. Louis had become less active in the Church and would not be able to participate in this ordinance at the present time, but he was made aware that he too could be sealed to this union. Gary and Lynn both accepted their mother's decision with good feelings. They may have been in shock, but they did not question this decision. Forgiveness and peace of mind came easily to each of them. As soon as Lynn could make the trip up from Panguitch, arrangements were made for these sealings to take place in the Salt Lake Temple.

Before this work could be performed, a lot of love and forgiveness had to take place. Lucile had to forgive Leo for the things she experienced because of him—his irresponsibility, drinking, and decision to abandon his family. Also, Lynn and Gary had to completely forgive their father for being absent throughout their entire lives, and for being instrumental in causing the trials and sufferings they witnessed in their mother's life. Leo himself would have to forgive himself and fully repent. He must have gone through great sorrow for the foolish and selfish earthly desires he had allowed to rule him. Looking now from the other side of the veil, he must have hungered for forgiveness and love from the only people who could bring him true exaltation.

On April 22, 1999, Lucile went with her two sons, Gary and Lynn, to the temple, and they were all sealed to Robert Leo Sagers as a family unit. Though Louis was unable to come, he called his mother from Florida that day and told her how happy he was for her. Someday, the family feels in their hearts, Louis will also be sealed into the family of Robert Leo and Lucile Embley Sagers.

At this special occasion in the temple, Lucile asked her oldest grandson, Steven Sagers, to stand in as a proxy for his grandfather Leo. Before Steve did so, he made several trips to the Tooele area, where Leo spent his childhood, and where Leo's parents had lived, and finally to the cemetery where they are all buried. Steven said he felt sure that Leo wanted this work to be done and that he had accepted the ordinances on his behalf.

About a month later, Lucile was back in the hospital again. Her health was deteriorating quickly now. Needing constant care, she made the decision to move into a nursing home. One day, when Gary and his wife, Carma, visited Lucile in the nursing home, Lucile told Carma about a dream she had. In this dream, Lucile saw the figure of a man in the room. She looked at him intently. It was Leo—a man with humble joy on his face.

Lucile knew that she would soon be crossing the veil. This dream reminded her that someone would be waiting for her. Though she did not go at this moment, she knew that when the time came she would go with joy, for Leo was holding his arms out to her.

Just three months after the sealings, on July 28, 1999, Lucile quietly slipped from this earth to go on her greatest and most exciting journey. At last her work was finished. We felt certain that a multitude of family and friends were eagerly awaiting her arrival and joyfully welcoming her home.

"Do My Ordinance Work"

by Jean Marshall

As a tiny child in Norway, little Oline began to have memorable dreams. One of the dreams she had was about leaving on a large ship. Once she fell asleep in a meadow overlooking a fjord. She dreamed that the sea rose up to the top of the cliff, bearing a great ship with sails of colorful silk. All the people on the ship beckoned to her to come aboard, but her brother Martin woke her, pulling her leg and scolding her. "You could have rolled in your sleep, over and over, down the slope to the edge of the cliff!"

She didn't climb aboard the big ship for many years. When she was five years old her mother died, and it was a hardship on her family. Her stern older sister, Ingeborg, insisted that Oline go with her to work in the port city of Bergen to help make ends meet. It was while they were in Bergen that they met two young men who had an important message for them—they were Mormon missionaries. The message was true. They knew it was true. Longing to go on the big ship across the sea to the land where the Church was strong, they continued to work to make their dream come true—to save enough money to go to Utah.

As Oline and Ingeborg continued to work hard, on one particular night, their mother came to Oline in a dream. In this dream, her mother told her that she must be the first to go to America and do the ordinance work for her in the Salt Lake Temple.

Oline was surprised. She was surprised at the clarity of the dream, and at her mother's request. She saw that her mother was aware that she and her sister had joined the Church, and now her mother was asking for something she wanted very much. However, Oline was still very young and hadn't yet saved enough money to take the ship she had seen once in her childhood dream.

Shaking, Oline replied that she did not have enough money to take such a trip to America. She had been working hard to accumulate that money, but she was far from her goal. It was true that her older sister Ingeborg had more money because she had been working longer and had been saving with great restraint. Oline mentioned that Ingeborg might have enough savings.

"Ask Ingeborg to help you, then," the mother said in a soft tone.

Because she was the younger sister, Oline had never had much success asking the tightfisted Ingeborg for anything. As a matter of fact, Ingeborg seldom listened to her younger sister at all. "You ask her yourself," Oline told her mother.

It was not long before Oline had another dream—a dream similar to the one in which she had been unable to get onto the ship. When she woke that morning, she wondered what would happen now.

She did not have to wait long. Ingeborg, yawning and stretching, came to the doorway and told Oline, "I had a dream last night. . . ."

It was another miraculous dream!

So, as things worked out, Oline did sail for America. When she reached Boston Harbor and they asked her for her name, she told them "Linchen" Steffensen, which was the diminutive for Oline Steffensen. But the American ears heard "Lincoln." My grandmother was proud of her new American name and used it throughout her life.

In Salt Lake City, Lincoln ran into Rudolph Stockseth, a man she had met in Norway some years before. She told me that even though another Norwegian girl who "laughed too loud" had eyes for Rudoph, Oline set her cap for him. "I was very pretty," she told me, "and I could make him laugh."

Rudoph and Lincoln married in the Salt Lake Temple, where

they soon afterward did the ordinance work for her mother. They also saved money carefully to repay Ingeborg and then to send for her and Oline's other sisters and brothers.

My mother had saved some of Lincoln's letters to us that she wrote when we moved to California. Though she uses English, the pages are generously sprinkled with Norwegian words. The spidery writing reminds me of the brusque woman and her abrupt, broken English, the bright red sweaters from her knitting needles, and the pungent aroma in her brown brick home of *surakal*—a tangy simmered dish of red cabbage, vinegar, sugar, and cloves.

Now when I look up at the Rocky Mountains, I think of her. Lincoln loved the mountains around the Salt lake Valley because they reminded her of Norway and helped to heal her homesickness for the majestic fjords. And when I run my finger over her name on a copy of the ship's list, I breathe sea air.

I Found My Dad

by Serge M. Ainsa

*I*n 1950—a few days before Christmas, when I was six years old and living in Palma de Mallorca, Spain—I stood on our living room balcony and watched a boat leave the shore. On board were my father and brother. With me on the balcony were my mother and sister. My father, a chemist of perfumes, was leaving to pursue opportunities in Uruguay, South America. He never returned. Several years later, he and my mother were divorced.

In the years that followed, I rarely heard from him. In the meantime, my mother took us to her native country, France, where in 1964 I was baptized a member of The Church of Jesus Christ of Latter-day Saints. One year later, I left France for Brigham Young University. In time, I served a mission, pursued graduate studies, and married.

Although my father had been almost completely out of my thoughts up to this point in my life, soon after my marriage a desire to do genealogical work for my ancestors began to bring him to my mind more and more often. My patriarchal blessing told me that the time would come for me to do the work for my ancestors through genealogy and temple ordinances and that "means and opportunities" would be provided for me to accomplish that work.

After I had joined the Church, my brother, who by then had moved to France, informed me that my father had accumulated facts, names, and dates on the Ainsa family. I resolved to write to my father, hoping to gain the necessary information about my grandparents and my paternal great-grandparents. I sent him a letter asking for details.

His reply consisted of a letter with only general information, nothing concrete, and a request that I not bother him again. I felt resentful and angry, but I continued to pray that the "means and opportunities" necessary to do my family history work would be provided.

Sometime in March 1986, while we were living in Arizona, my father wrote again during a family crisis in which my mother was losing her sight. I was comforted by the care and concern that my mother's second husband showed her and was again offended at my father's critical letter. I sent it back to him and indicated that if I couldn't receive pleasant letters instead of criticism, I would rather not communicate at all. Within three weeks my father answered the letter, telling me, "Your brother will inform you of my passing when it occurs. I don't intend to write again."

Nine months passed after I received the letter. Again I prayed about the admonition in my patriarchal blessing. The answer came unmistakably from the Spirit—I felt I should apologize to my father. I consequently composed a five-page letter to him that detailed the events of the year and included an apology for my erratic behavior reflected in my previous letter. When I mailed the letter, I prayed that the Lord would soften my father's heart.

Almost two and one-half months went by with no answer, until one day a registered letter arrived. In it, my father asked, "Would you spare ten to twelve days during your upcoming summer vacation to visit me? If you accept, I will send you the money to defray your expenses."

I called my brother in Paris, France, who suggested that I wait a year, since my father had waited thirty-five years to try to see me. But as I prayed with my wife, Angie, we both thought of my patriarchal blessing and knew that my ancestors had waited long enough. I would go this year—a decision that was wholly confirmed by subsequent events that provided the "opportunity and means" to discover the records of my paternal ancestors. My mother's husband offered to pay for Angie's trip, as we couldn't afford it ourselves. My mother-in-law offered to care for our four children in her home in California.

Everything went according to schedule—everything, that is, except my feelings of apprehension. I started worrying that my father might criticize my mother, my wife, or me. He had done it before. How would I handle it this time?

Only when two dedicated home teachers—to whom I will be eternally grateful—came to our home a few days before our departure and gave us each a priesthood blessing did I feel at peace. They blessed my wife that she would be a source of inspiration to me, and they blessed me that I would be receptive to the promptings of the Spirit and would know what to say. I then knew that everything would be all right.

When we arrived in Montevideo, Uruguay, I nervously looked for my father and saw him standing behind a window with his wife. He waved his cane at me. I waved back. Finally, the customs officer told me to proceed. As I walked through the customs door, my father eagerly came toward me. We embraced and kissed each other. As we left the terminal, the Spirit told me that the man walking beside me was a different person from what I had imagined.

We spent the next few days getting acquainted with one another, laughing together, discovering what we had in common, and becoming friends. Angie and I asked him to record on tape his experiences in youth and in courting my mother, and we discovered many things about his past. Then, one morning, Angie and I prayed that we would be blessed with the right words to ask my father to share with us the Ainsa genealogy and history.

It was my father's eighty-first birthday. After opening presents at breakfast, he excused himself and came back with an object hidden underneath a towel. He handed me a box and said, "This is the least I can do after all these years. Somehow, I feel that I have to make it up to you." Inside the box was a beautiful watch.

Thirty minutes later, as we were upstairs, sitting around my father's oak desk, I inserted a blank tape into the cassette recorder and asked him to tell me about my ancestors. He talked for a few minutes, then stopped. "It's a waste," he said.

I panicked. "Lord, please help me," I prayed. "I've been wait-ing for this moment for years." Then I asked my father, "Why do you say it is a waste?"

"Because I have it in print," he replied. My heart began to beat faster as he reached for a drawer in his desk, opened it, pulled out a folder, and handed me a sheet of paper with a list of names on it. "These are your ancestors on my father's side," he said. "And you're welcome to this list." I glanced quickly through it. It con-tained the names of his parents and his father's parents, grandpar-ents, and great-grandparents, as well as those of distant relatives.

"What about your mother? Have you compiled a list on her?" I asked, my voice trembling.

"Your grandmother's lineage is not important," he muttered, brushing aside my inquiry. I replied that were it not for my grand-mother, he wouldn't be here. "Well, if it is that important to you, you can have it." With that, he gave me an envelope containing names scribbled on several sheets of paper and said, "As a matter of fact, you might as well have everything." He placed the folder in my hands.

I opened it and, as tears began to blur my vision, I read through several lists of names of distant relatives. Inside were pictures of my grandmother, my grandfather, and others. I wept openly. During the past twenty-one years I had prayed on many occasions for this day. The Lord had heard my requests and had answered them at the appropriate time.

"Why are you crying?" my father asked.

"Because I am happy to be here," I said.

At that moment, he too began to cry. He leaned his head on my shoulder and took my hand between his. "I am sorry," he said. "I am sorry for what I did. I was wrong. I was never a father to you. During all those years I never bothered to find out who you were. Will you ever forgive me?"

"Of course I forgive you—it is forgiven and forgotten," I uttered between sobs. As I embraced him, the Spirit whispered softly, "I, the Lord will forgive whom I will forgive, but of you it is required to forgive all men" (D&C 64:10).

We were at peace. All the years of separation, loneliness and turmoil melted away. He knew who I was. He had found a son. And I had finally found my dad.

"I Found My Dad," by Serge Ainsa.
Copyright Intellectual Reserve, Inc.
First published in the *Ensign*, April 1990.

Grandmother's Treasures

by Joyce Baggerly

"*T*his box of pictures and my purse are the only things I
saved in the 1937 Ohio River flood," my grandmother had
told me many times.

As a child, I had loved sitting by her knee as she told me
about the pictures she had managed to save. Though at that time
neither she nor I had any idea I would be the one who would want
to write family histories someday, she had written on the box that
I was to inherit these treasures when she died. Now I had a vital
interest in them. So, this time, when she told me about what she'd
managed to save during that devastating flood, I was sitting at her
kitchen table in Evansville, Indiana, prepared to fully document
every picture.

We worked for several hours. My grandmother talked about
the pictures as I recorded her memories. Even as we stopped to
have lunch, we continued our labor of love. At one point, my
grandmother picked up a baby picture. "That's Beatrice Rhodes,"
she reminisced.

"Who?" I asked. I had never heard that name before.

"Beatrice Rhodes. She died when I was a little girl. I remember going to her funeral."

I wanted to know if she was one of the Warrick County
Rhodeses.

"Oh yes. She was my first cousin. Her father and my father
were brothers."

A cousin. I had many questions. "What did she die of?"

"Meningitis," my grandmother said in a soft voice.

I wanted to know what she remembered.

"The thing I remember most was seeing her standing up, holding onto the back of a chair. It was the least painful way for her to be. She died still holding onto that chair."

"Poor little girl." I felt such sorrow for her.

"I think she was at least six or seven years old," my grandmother continued. "I remember our mother made us take naps every summer day because she didn't want us to get sick like Cousin Beatrice. That was the only way they knew to prevent meningitis."

"Did she have siblings?" I asked.

"No, they never had any other children."

One little child—a cousin—who had died of meningitis. But I had never seen a tombstone for her in all of the times we'd been in the cemeteries in Warrick County. "Where was she buried?" I asked.

My grandmother paused. "I would guess she was buried on the family farm with the babies who only lived a few hours or days. So many children died back then that the families just buried them quietly on the farm."

I was stunned. The babies had never made it to the cemetery. And I knew that the farm had been strip-mined fifty years before. I wondered if those graves had been moved? But my grandmother didn't think they had. The babies had been buried without tombstones. She said, "I played there as a child and I don't remember any markers. I haven't thought about her in years."

No wonder I had never heard of little Beatrice Rhodes. There was no marked grave. It was as though she had been swept out of the family.

I felt so sad. I was determined that when I got back to Utah I would see what I could find out about her. But when I began my search for any reference at all to Beatrice, I hit one blank wall after another. My grandmother had been born in 1894, so I reasoned that Beatrice would have been born about 1890. But much of the 1890 U.S. Census was destroyed in a fire in 1921, so I couldn't rely on a census. Vital records did not exist either.

I spent an entire day in the Family History Library in Salt Lake City looking for this little girl, but I found nothing.

On my next visit to Indiana, my grandmother and I went to Warrick County to see what local sources we could find. There was nothing there either.

The next day, we decided to visit some of the older family members to see if they remembered Beatrice. We hoped we could get other Rhodes family stories at the same time. Our day was pleasant, and we accomplished many family history projects. We gathered material from several of the older family members who remembered vividly that Beatrice always stood up, holding on to the back of a chair. They were sure that she had been buried on the family farm, probably in a coffin her father and his brothers had made. But no one had any idea of how old she had been, nor the exact year she had died.

Over the years, I continued to search for references to this child. If her parents had no other children, then there was no one left to prove she belonged in our family. I was bent on continuing my search until I found some proof—for as long as it took.

Some twenty years after my grandmother and I had gone through her box of pictures, the U.S. 1900 Census was released for public use. I wanted to see what I could find in that census.

Two columns on that census were of great interest to me. The two columns stood out as though they had somehow been marked. The first was "Mother of how many children" and the second was "Number of these children living." As soon as I realized those two columns were there, I quickly searched for Beatrice's parents. Sure enough, Beatrice's mother was there. In the first column under "Mother of how many children," there was a "1." And when I looked in the column under "Number of these children living" I saw a "0."

I had found Beatrice! Her mother was correctly documented, and there was one child, deceased!

Now, with the little baby picture of her in my hand, and the information from the 1900 U.S. Census about her mother, I was secure with my grandmother's memories. Now Beatrice is where she belongs—securely tucked into the history of the Rhodes family of Warrick County, Indiana.

Cristel in the Light

by Pat L. Sagers

*S*ometimes it was hard to know why he awoke over an hour before his alarm went off. But it happened to him this winter morning.

It was pitch dark and deadly cold in Moroni, Utah, that time of year. He could hear the heater struggling to blow air through the house. He heard the snow shifting on the roof. He lay awake, listening, wondering if his sheep would freeze. He knew that northwest of Moroni, in the fields just south of Jericho, his herds were huddling against the storm. He thought he ought to check on them. While he may be enjoying a semiwarm bed, he knew that they might be in trouble.

Quiet, so as not to wake his father, Roger Cook got out of bed, pulled on his clothes, grabbed his flashlight, and tiptoed into the kitchen. But his father must have heard him. There he was in the kitchen, his hair disheveled, his eyes still half shut from sleep.

"What's the matter?" his father asked. "Why are you going so early? It's not even 4:00 yet."

"I'm just worried about my sheep in the snowstorm," Roger replied.

His father, concerned, realized that his eighteen-year-old son was protective of the first sheep that were really his. He rubbed his hair and turned to go back to bed. "Just be careful driving on this ice in the dark."

On his way out, Roger read the temperature. It was seventeen degrees below zero. Everything on the truck was so cold he couldn't touch it without gloves. On the road out of Moroni going toward Nephi and out to Eureka, it was so dark and foggy that all Roger could see was the white line in the middle of the road. He kept his eye on the line and moved slowly northwest in the darkness until, illuminated by the headlights, he saw something humped over in the road.

He wasn't sure if it was an animal. It was a strange shape for any animal he had ever seen. It looked like a girl.

As his headlights moved forward, the creature crawled off the road and just rolled off the edge. And as he passed whatever it was, he thought he saw a puddle of blood. As the truck continued down the road, a dread shook him. He knew he ought to go back and see if he could help this woman.

He stopped the truck, made a U-turn and drove back. At first, he could see nothing there. He got out of the truck and went to the borrow pit. When he looked down into it, he could see a figure lying there. Yes, it was a woman! He couldn't believe it. And she looked frozen cold. All she had on was a dress with spaghetti straps. Her arms and shoulders were bare. Apparently she had been to a dance that Saturday evening of January 11, 1964. It was now early Sunday morning, January 12, at about 4:20 A.M.

When the woman had rolled off the road to avoid the truck, she had landed in brush. When Roger knelt to untangle her from the brush, he could see that she was barely alive. Her eyes were open, but she was unable to say a word. When he tried to pick her up to carry her to the truck, her arms were so stiff with cold that he had to bend them to fit her inside. They remained straight out in front of her in a Z shape.

Roger looked around. Here was a woman frozen with cold, almost dead, and there was no one in sight.

* * *

The above narrative is the story that Roger Cook told about finding Cristel Sagers, but my husband and I (Lynn and Pat Sagers) also "found" Cristel Sagers.

101

Our story begins one day in January many years later, when we received a phone call from a woman who introduced herself as Norma Sherwood. She said that she had a story she wanted to tell us about a Sagers woman, and she wondered if this woman might be related to us. The name Sagers was not a common name. Yes, we were interested, we told her. So we made arrangements to go to her home on January 20, 2001.

Norma was a bright, articulate, lovely lady, who was ninety-one years young in 2001. Married to a Utah highway patrolman, she spent much of her life chasing news stories and writing them up for newspapers and magazines. Norma told us that a short time ago she just happened to be going through the Nephi telephone book looking at the names of people, surprised at how many new people had moved into the area. She happened to come across the Sagers name. We had been in the area for one year, but the name Sagers was important to her. She had never forgotten it. Thirty-seven years ago, she had written a story about a woman named Cristel Sagers.

We had never heard of Cristel Sagers, but we had a Sagers family history book, and found her listed as Sterling Sagers's wife. Sterling was Lynn's uncle—his father Robert Leo's half brother. Lynn had never been very close to the Sagers family since his mother and father had divorced when he was just a toddler. But now we knew that Cristel was Lynn's aunt. And of course we were interested in Norma's story.

Norma explained to us that the only articles that appeared in the newspapers were two short ones that basically described the automobile accident. Soon after Cristel was released from the hospital, Norma drove to Lynndyl, where Cristel was staying with her parents, to get the whole story. She found it so fascinating that she wrote it up and took photographs. Finally she gave the negatives to a Mr. Brunaman, who was going to have it published in a magazine. However, Mr. Brunaman moved out of state, and the story and the negatives were returned to Norma. The story was never published.

As we sat on Norma's sofa, she pulled up a stool and sat in

front of us holding a large pink envelope marked "Cristel Sagers." The pages she drew out were old, yellowed, and folded in fourths with tears along the folded lines. Patiently, Norma answered our questions and set the scene for the story by explaining that when Mrs. Sagers had been brought to the hospital, everyone thought she was dying. She was in critical condition from frostbite.

We sat enthralled as Norma first read the letter to Mr. Brunaman, and finally the story she had written from the interview of Cristel Sagers.

* * *

February 7, 1964
Dear Mr. Brunaman:

I assume you have the original newspaper account of the Sagers accident, so I will just continue on with the story as you requested. If there are other questions you'd like answered I may or may not be able to answer them. But I will hope that I can. I think this is about as complete a story as I can get from Mrs. Sagers.

I visited Mrs. Sagers in Lynndyl, Utah, yesterday, in the little modest frame home of her parents, Mr. and Mrs. Ivin Nielson. Cristel Nielson Sagers has been living with her parents since separating some time ago from her husband, Sterling, with whom she had spent ten years of married life. She and her husband have no children. However, they are not divorced. Her husband has been living in Salt Lake City and they have been seeing one another—perhaps in the hopes of reconciliation.

The experience I had interviewing Mrs. Sagers was a very valuable one to me—I shall remember it the rest of my life. Cristel sat on the edge of her couch and relived for me in detail the story of a torturous and horrible experience that—save for a miracle—would have caused her to be frozen to death. As a news correspondent I had covered the tragic accident some four weeks earlier. But now I was asking her if she would relive the story again for me in every difficult detail.

Cristel Sagers, age thirty, dressed in a cotton housecoat, is a very slender, frail blond woman with large blue eyes. All the toes on her right foot and three toes on her left are heavily bandaged. She kept the fingers on both hands spread wide apart, as the skin was very tender, sensitive, and red. Her fingernails were gone, and new ones were beginning to form. She seemed a little hesitant to talk, but finally opened up to me.

"Norma, I don't know what else I can tell you that you don't already know," she said in a quiet voice. "Unless I tell you what *really* saved me. But . . ."

My pen was poised and I was curious.

"But it is a sacred and wonderful experience. And I don't know if you want that."

I said, "Of course I want it."

She replied, "This part of my experience is to me the *only* part that is important. Without this spiritual experience, the entire event means nothing!"

By now I was very curious. I didn't know whether to speak and interrupt her thoughts or to be silent. I chose to be silent.

"It is about my twenty-six-year-old brother, Gary; I didn't tell you about him. He died a year and a half ago."

I had heard about Gary's death. But I didn't know how much he meant to Cristel until I heard her story. It is a story that seems to testify of the importance of family. This is the way Cristel told it to me, Mr. Brunaman, and I am willing to share it with you and with others who might be interested, if you would like.

Sincerely,
Norma Sherwood

* * *

One Saturday night—January 11, 1964—my husband Sterling and I drove to Delta to go to a dance. We had a good time. I remember feeling glad to be at a party again. I hadn't done much celebrating since my brother's death four months earlier. I missed him. While I was a bit of a reprobate, he had been a good member of the Church, always conscientious. I had felt how unfair it was that he had died such a terrible death in the hospital with tubes in his arms.

When the party was over early Sunday morning, about 2:30 A.M., Sterling and I drove east in his 1952 Olds. We were both in good humor. The weather was bitter cold and skiffs of fog kept drifting across the road. Though the road was dry, there was about a foot of snow on either side of it. Official weather records showed that it was about fifteen to twenty degrees below zero in that area that night.

When we were about twelve miles west of Nephi on Highway 132, at about 3:00 A.M., Sterling suddenly looked over at me to say something, and then yelled, "Look out! Hold on!"

I knew the car was leaving the road. Rushing toward me at a rapid speed were flurries of gutted snowdrifts and the branches of cedar trees. Bang! My head crashed against the door window next to me. That was the last thing I remembered for a while.

When I came to, I felt all closed in. I could tell the car was upside down. I was numb and dazed, but I tried to get out on the driver's side, as that door was open. The steering wheel was jammed near the seat and I couldn't get out that way. I had no pain. I wasn't feeling much of anything. I could hear Sterling. He sounded far away, and he was calling my name.

I felt around in the darkness and found that the window glass on my side was broken. So I crawled out of the jagged hole. While I was getting out, a car passed along the highway. I screamed to them, but they did not hear me. And they couldn't have seen us as we were off the road some twenty feet. We had slid down an embankment.

Both sides of my face felt hard to my touch. I thought my skin must be encrusted with snow. But I later learned it was blood that had frozen on my face from the deep, four-inch gash over my right forehead, which had bled profusely. The doctor said later that this cake of blood on my face had actually protected me during the ordeal which was to follow.

I tried to get around the car to find my husband. I finally

found him in the snow about fifteen feet from the front of the car. Though he was still calling for me, he was mostly unconscious. He kept saying, "Oh, Cris! Oh, Cris!" Then he would lapse into unconsciousness again.

I took off my coat to cover him up. Though my narrow-strapped party dress was wool and I had on wool-lined snow boots, my head and arms were bare. I knew it was terribly cold, but in the state of semishock I was functioning in, it didn't seem to matter how cold it was. I felt numb. After I covered Sterling with my coat, I ducked into the wreck to search for the quilt and sleeping bag I remembered we had in the car. I had to tramp a long way around in the snow to get into the backseat, as both back doors had been broken. While I was there, Sterling came stumbling around the car to me. I made him get into the back part of the upside-down car, thinking he'd be more protected from the cold. As soon as he got inside, he vomited blood and passed out again. Finally I got him covered with my coat and the quilt, and had him partially stuffed into the sleeping bag. All this time I was watching for cars, but no cars seemed to be passing at 3:00 A.M. at all.

When Sterling came to again, I told him that I was going to walk for help. I thought we were closer to Nephi than we were. It was later that I learned we were twelve miles away. Sterling had another suggestion. He told me to help him move away from the car and set fire to it so that we could get warm.

But with my husband going in and out of consciousness, I felt I had to go. When he fell unconscious again, I struggled with the decision of what we should do. For about twenty minutes, I tried to make up my mind. I tried to feel his heartbeat. I could feel it beating feebly. It was then that I decided to try to walk to Nephi for help.

It was when I left Sterling's warm side that I realized how cold my hands were. I found my gloves and tried to put them on. I got the left one on, but the right one wouldn't budge, my hand was so stiff. It was then that I put the quilt over my head and shoulders and stumbled in the dark, through the snow, through the tangled underbrush and cedar trees.

When I got to the road I thought that if I sat on the edge, at least someone might *see* me. It was a few minutes before I knew which direction to take. It was so foggy that I could barely see the white line in the middle of the road. When I managed to reach the top of the hill, I started down the other side. I kept squatting down so that the quilt would warm my legs. The third time I did this I couldn't get up again. I fell over. Then, as I was just sitting there in the cold I heard a voice.

"Well, Sis, you've got yourself in a mess, haven't you?" I looked up and saw my brother Gary.

Standing above me, he was wearing his white shirt, open at the throat, as I had always remembered him. He was dressed in white pants.

I said, "Gary! You shouldn't be out here in the cold without a coat!"

He said, "Cold weather don't bother me." Then he laughed. He told me that if I didn't get up and keep moving, I'd freeze.

I told him I had tried to get up, but that I couldn't seem to stand.

He said, "I can't touch you. But if you'll reach up your hand to me, I'll give you the strength to get up."

I reached up my hand toward him and I was able to have the strength to get to my feet. When I looked at the hand he had reached down to me, I thought about the tubes he had in his arm when he died. I said, "Gary, where are the tubes that were in your arm?"

"They were only in my body," he said.

For what seemed like a long time, I walked along beside my brother. We talked and visited. I told him what had been happening in the family and gave him other tidbits of news. He always answered by saying, "Yes, I know. I know."

It seemed so natural that my brother was there with me. It was like a dream. Yet I knew that I was awake. I remember worrying about Sterling, and how much I wanted my brother to help my husband also. It was so awfully cold. And I was so tired.

I knew I was walking because I could hear my feet on the road. But I couldn't feel my feet or legs at all. I said to my brother, "It's funny, I can't feel my legs and feet. But I can hear my feet walking!"

He replied: "That's all right, as long as you keep moving."

As we talked about many things, Gary finally told me, "This experience had to happen to you. You weren't listening."

It's true I hadn't been listening. Gary had always wanted me to be a little more active in the Church. But my husband and I had been wayward. We had been thinking of our parties, and of many other less important things.

I did ask Gary what it was like where he was. He said that he was happier and busier than he had ever been in his life. When I asked him how he felt about his wife, who had remarried after his death, he said, "I thought it was wonderful. I was happy. But I had a hard time to convince them it was the right thing to do." He had wanted her to remarry, to have a pleasant life. And evidently he had been instrumental in making it happen.

As we walked along, my brother wouldn't let me sit down and rest. He would let me stand a while—then he'd say, "Come on, let's go now."

I told him I was still worried about my husband back there alone. But he said, "Don't worry about Sterling. His mother is with him." Later I asked my husband if he had been aware of his mother's presence, but he told me no.

The last thing I remember was that I was so tired I wanted to sit down and rest. I asked my brother, "Can't I go with you?"

He said, "Oh, Sis, you can't leave a job half done!"

I don't remember sitting down or falling down, but the next thing I remembered was a bright light coming toward me. I thought Gary was relenting and that he would take me with him.

But the bright lights were the headlights of a truck driven by Mr. Roger Cook, eighteen years old, a sheep rancher from Moroni, in Sanpete County, Utah, who was on his way to the sheep herd by Jericho, west of Nephi about thirty-five miles. It was 5:40 A.M., still dark, and still bitterly cold. Mr. Cook, traveling west on the highway, passed an object on the road that looked like an animal. It was me, crawling on my hands and knees down the road. When he turned the truck around and came back to investigate, at first he could not find anything. To get out of the way of the lights, I had backed up to the side of the road and catapulted into the borrow pit.

When he saw me, Mr. Cook said it nearly scared him to death. He had to extricate me from the tangled brush. When he touched my hair he thought it would break off, it was so stiff! He said my arms were so frozen he had to take both of his hands to bend my arms to get me into his truck. The quilt must have dropped off in the borrow pit. He said there was no blanket. He wrapped me in a sheepskin vest and raced back with me to the Juab County Hospital in Nephi. I was unable to speak except just to say I had been in an accident.

Mr. Cook told me later on that he had been unable to sleep that night. He had started out to go to the sheep herd at Jericho one and one-half hours to two hours earlier than usual. Had he been traveling the road at his usual time, he would have been too late!

Mr. Cook located the Juab County sheriff, Raymond Jackson, and Highway Patrol Trooper Rex Hill, and guided them out along the highway to the point where he had found me. At first the officers suspected Mr. Cook of foul play, until they proceeded further along the road about four miles, where they located the accident scene and found my husband. Sterling had revived and set fire to the seat cushions of the car. He was sitting by the fire. The sheriff and the trooper brought my husband back to the Nephi hospital, where they thought I was dying.

I didn't regain consciousness until about 9:00 A.M. Sunday morning. From the moment I revived, I began a slow, torturous recovery. The doctors said they expected me to die, but it would be twenty-four hours before they could tell which way things would go.

That afternoon, eight hours after I entered the hospital, a

cheery, outgoing journalist came to ask me about my story. Her name was Norma Sherwood. Married to a Utah highway patrolman, she was good at getting the facts about accidents, crime scenes, and local news. She took photographs of me and told me she believed I was going to get better. I had a feeling I would get better too.

The doctor said I had suffered frozen feet and hands—also, a frozen nose, which was black and swollen. My knees were black and bleeding. My feet and fingers were black. The doctor said that if I lived, he was sure he would have to amputate my feet. He said I would have to stay in the hospital for months. The gash on my forehead had required about twenty stitches to close. I had been exposed to below zero weather for four or five hours and had walked and crawled on the highway for a distance of four miles!

Upon examination, Sterling was found to have suffered slightly frosted toes and slight chest bruises. He was released from the hospital in six days.

It was three days before the feeling came back into my legs, feet, and hands. The pain was terrific, in spite of the pain-killing drugs I was given. But I was in the hospital just eighteen days! The doctor said he'd stopped making predictions. He said, "I just don't believe my eyes!" He joked, asking me if I would like to go through this again, and I said, "For the same wonderful spiritual experience, I'd do it again."

He didn't wait around to hear my story. But he gave me a bit of advice. "Well, don't try it. Next time you might not be so lucky!"

Mrs. Sherwood came to get a more complete story just twenty-six days after the accident. I had gone home to be cared for by my loving mother, making frequent trips back to the hospital in Nephi for check-ups. The doctor's prognosis at this time was that I might have to have the tips of a couple of toes amputated.

I cannot explain how honored I feel to be on this earth. I am anxious to return to teach my Nursery class in Sunday School. I also teach the Mia Maids in the MIA, and accompany the singing mothers' chorus in the Lynndyl LDS ward. During the week,

I hope to continue clerking in the little Lynndyl general store. I also pray that my husband and I will be able to get together again sometime in the future. I am so grateful for the siblings who care for me now: Ivie, thirty-two years old, Leon, twenty-eight, and Karen, twenty.

I was spared to "listen better" and to "find my way," and perhaps to share this wonderful spiritual experience with others.

* * *

Cristel and Sterling's story left a great impression on my husband, Lynn Sagers, and me. As we went over all of the facts behind this story, we felt that there was more than mere coincidence to the events surrounding our discovery of Cristel Sagers. It had been like finding a hidden treasure. There are several facts that are worth describing:

1. Norma Sherwood, ninety-one-year-old author of the story, seems to be a miracle in and of herself. The fact that she wrote the story thirty-seven years ago; the fact that she carefully kept it and the photograph negatives in her files; and the fact that she kept Cristel's name and the story alive in her memory so that she would pick the name "Sagers" out of the phone book are all amazing occurrences.

2. We, Pat and Lynn Sagers, had moved to Nephi, Utah, only a year ago. Our name was left out of the phone book the first year we were there. It had just barely been added to the new edition when Norma Sherwood found us.

3. Norma was studying the phone book for no reason, but just happened to remember the name Sagers when she saw us listed there.

4. After hearing the story from Norma, we went home, pulled out our genealogy books, and took a good look at Lynn's Grandpa Sagers and both of his wives and their families. After looking at our records, we realized that Lynn's two uncles—Sterling and Joseph—never had any children of their own. They also both had died without having their temple work done. And everyone

111

in the family, it seems, had forgotten them. Also, Lynn's aunt Zona Faye had a family, but no one had done her temple work yet either. This information has now been put on TempleReady software, and those necessary ordinances will soon be done. Zona Faye's daughter said that they would like to do their work, so the cards have been mailed to her.

We aren't sure what meaning this will bring to Cristel and her family. But we feel that Cristel also needs to have this chapter out of her own life's story for a particular reason at this time.

After listening to Cristel testify that her brother Gary Nielson and Sterling's mother, Clara Edna Sagers, were willing to help them through a difficult earthly situation, it's easier to understand the concern of those who have gone before as they hover over their loved ones here on earth. Our families across the veil seem to be trying to get us to "listen."

The Work That Goes On

by Heber Q. Hale

*I*t is only because I have been asked to do so that I relate a personal experience that is very sacred to me. It is with a humble and grateful spirit that I have decided to offer my story, praying that if I tell it, the reader will be inspired to understand it only in the context in which it is told, and that it will encourage good works.

On the night of January 20, 1920, while alone in a room at the home of my friend W. J. Brawson in Carey, Idaho, a glorious manifestation was given to me.

I was not conscious of anything that transpired that night except for this manifestation. I did not turn over in bed, nor was I disturbed by any sound, which is unusual for me. Whether it be called a dream, an apparition, a vision, or a pilgrimage of my spirit into the world of spirits I care not. I know I actually saw and experienced the things related regarding this heavenly manifestation, and they are as real to me as any experience in my life.

Of all the doctrines and practices of the Church, the vicarious work for the dead has been the most difficult for me to comprehend and wholeheartedly accept. I consider this vision the Lord's answer to the prayer of my soul on this and certain other questions.

I passed but a short distance from my body through a film into the world of spirits. This was my first experience after going to sleep. I seemed to realize that I had passed through the change called death. I mentioned this in my first conversation with the immortal beings with whom I immediately came in contact.

I immediately observed their displeasure at my use of the word "death" and their rejection of the fear that we attach to it. There they use another word in referring to the transition from mortality, although I cannot recall the word they used. I can only approach its meaning. The impression of the meaning it left upon my mind was "new birth."

My first visual impression was the nearness of the world of spirits to the world of mortality. The vastness of this heavenly sphere was bewildering to the eyes of my spirit. Many of those I saw enjoyed unrestricted freedom of both vision and action. The vegetation and landscape was beautiful beyond description, like the rainbow, not all green, but gold, with various shades of pink, orange, and lavender. A sweet calmness pervaded everything. I had a sense of the people I met there not as spirits, but as men and women—self-thinking, self-acting individuals going about important business in a most orderly manner. There was perfect order, as a matter of fact. Everyone had something to do and seemed to be about their business.

I learned that the inhabitants of the spirit world are classified according to how they lived and their obedience to the Father's will. Particularly, I observed that the wicked and unrepentant are confined to a certain district by themselves, the confines of which are as definitely determined and impassable as the line marking the division of the physical and spiritual world—a mere film, but impassable until the person himself has changed. The world of spirits is the temporary abode of all spirits, pending the resurrection from the dead and the judgment.

There was much activity within the different spheres, and I saw appointed ministers coming from the higher to the lower places in pursuit of their missionary appointments.

I had a pronounced desire to meet certain of my kinfolk and friends, but I was at once impressed with the fact that I had entered a tremendously great and extensive world, even greater than our earth and more numerously inhabited. I could be in only one place at a time, could look in only one direction at a time, and accordingly it would require many years to search out and converse with all those I had known and those whom I desired to meet, unless they were especially summoned to receive me.

All worthy men and women were appointed to special and regular work. There was a well-organized plan of action. It was directed principally toward preaching the gospel to the unconverted, teaching those who sought knowledge, establishing family relationships, and gathering genealogies for the use and benefit of mortal relatives who were vicariously performing baptisms and sealing ordinances for the departed in the temples on earth.

The authorized representatives of families in the world of spirits have access to our temple records and are kept fully advised of the work therein. But the vicarious work done by mortals does not become automatically effective unless the recipients first repent and accept baptism and confirmation. Then certain consummating ordinances are performed in the spirit world.

So the great work is going on. They are doing a work there that we cannot do here, and we are doing a work here that they cannot do. Both parts are necessary, each the compliment of the other. Thus, spirits and mortals are bringing about the salvation of all God's children who will be saved.

I was surprised to find there were no babes in arms. I met the infant son of Arson W. Rawlings, my first counselor, and immediately recognized him as the baby who had died a few years earlier. Yet he seemed to have the intelligence and the appearance of an adult. He was engaged in matters pertaining to his family and its genealogy.

My mind was quite content on the point that mothers will again receive into their arms their children who die in infancy and will be fully satisfied. The entrance into the world of spirits is not an inhibition of growth, but a great opportunity for development. Earthly babies are adult spirits in infant bodies.

I beheld a mighty multitude of men, the largest I have ever seen gathered in one place. I immediately recognized them as soldiers. They were the millions who had been savagely slaughtered and rushed into the world of spirits during the World Wars.

As I passed on, I met my beloved mother. She greeted me

affectionately and expressed surprise at seeing me there. She reminded me that I had not completed my allotted mission on earth. She seemed to be in a hurry to go somewhere and accordingly took her leave, saying she would see me again.

I moved forward, covering an appreciable distance and consuming considerable time viewing the wonderful landscapes, parks, trees, and flowers. I not only met many people I had known, but also many thousands I did not recognize.

Soon I approached a small group of men standing on a path lined with spacious stretches of flowers, grasses, and shrubbery, all of a golden hue. The path led to a beautiful building. The men were engaged in earnest conversation. One of their number parted from the rest and came walking down the path. I at once recognized former Church President Joseph F. Smith, whom I had known in the flesh. He embraced me as a father would embrace a son. And after a few words of greeting, he quickly remarked, "You have not come to stay."

For the first time I became fully aware of my incomplete mission on earth. And as much as I would like to have remained, I at once asked President Smith if I might return to earth.

"You have expressed a righteous desire," he replied, "and I shall take the matter up with the authorities and let you know later." He then turned and led me toward the little gathering of men from whom he had just separated. I immediately recognized Brigham Young and the Prophet Joseph Smith. I was surprised to find Brother Young shorter and heavier than I expected. All three of these men were in possession of a calm and holy majesty, which was at once kind and kingly. President Smith introduced me to the others, who greeted me warmly. We then returned to our original place. President Smith took his leave, saying he would see me again.

From a certain vantage point, I was permitted to view this earth and what was going on here. There were no limitations to my vision and I was astonished at this. I saw my wife and children at home. I saw President Heber J. Grant at the head of the great Church and kingdom of God, and felt the divine power that radiated from God, giving the Church light and truth—guiding its destiny.

I beheld this nation, founded as it is upon correct principles and designed to endure even though evil and sinister forces seek to lead men astray and thwart the purposes of God. I saw towns and cities and the sin and wickedness of men and women. I saw vessels sailing upon the ocean and I scanned the battle-scarred fields of France and Belgium. I saw the whole world as if it were a panorama passing before my eyes.

Then there came to me the unmistakable impression that this earth and the persons upon it are open to the visions of the Spirit only when special permission is given or when they are assigned to special service. This is particularly true of the righteous who are busily engaged in the service of the Lord and cannot be engaged in two fields of activity at the same time.

Though the wicked and unrepentant spirits have their free agency, they apply themselves in no useful or wholesome undertaking, but seek pleasure in their old habits to the extent that they are still tools of Satan. It is idle, mischievous, and deceptive spirits who appear as miserable counterfeits at spiritualistic scenes, ouija boards, table dancing, and other such things. The noble and great men and women do not respond to the call of the mediums and every curious group of meddlesome inquirers. They would not do it in mortality and they certainly do not do it in their increased state of knowledge in the world of immortality. The wicked and unrepentant spirits are allies of Satan and his hosts operating through willing mediums in the flesh. These three forces constitute an unholy trinity upon the earth and all are responsible for wickedness among men and nations.

I moved forward, feasting my eyes upon the beauty. Everything about me was glowing in indescribable peace and happiness that abounded in everybody and in everything. The farther I went, the more glorious things appeared.

I beheld a short distance away a wonderfully beautiful temple. It was capped with golden domes. Coming from the temple was a small group of men dressed in robes, conversing with one another.

These were the first people I had seen dressed like this. The millions I had previously seen were dressed in different ways. The soldiers, for instance, were in uniforms.

In this little group of holy men, my eyes rested upon one more splendid and holy than all the rest. President Smith parted from the others and came to my side.

"Do you know him?" he asked. I quickly answered that I did. My eyes beheld the Lord and Savior. My soul was filled with a sudden, unspeakable joy.

President Smith informed me that I had been given permission to return and complete the mission that the Lord had appointed for me on the earth.

"Brother Heber, you have a great work to do," President Smith said, placing his hand on my shoulder. "Go forward with all your heart, and you shall be blessed in your mission. From this time on, never doubt that God lives, that Jesus Christ is his Son, the Redeemer of the world, and that the Holy Ghost is a God of spirit and the messenger for the Father and the Son. Never doubt the resurrection of the dead and the immortality of the soul." Having completed these remarks, he bade me farewell.

I traveled a considerable distance through various scenes and past innumerable people before I reached the sphere where I had first entered the world of spirits. I was greeted by many friends and relatives, some of whom sent words of greeting and counsel to dear ones on earth. My brother was one of them.

I will mention one other thing. I met Brother John Adamson, his wife, his son James, and his daughter Isabelle, all of whom were killed by the hand of an assassin in Carey, Idaho, on the evening of October 29, 1915. They seemed to divine that I was on my way back to mortality and immediately asked me to tell their children that they were happy, and not to mourn their departure or worry their minds over the manner in which they were taken.

"There is a purpose in it, and we have work here to do that requires our collective efforts, which we could not do individually," said Brother Adamson.

The work they were speaking of was genealogy. They were

working with the records in England and Scotland. One of the most sacred and remarkable projects of heaven is family relationships—the establishment of a complete chain without a broken link. The unholy will be dropped out and other new links put in, or two adjoining links welded together. Men and women throughout the world are moved upon by their dead ancestors to gather genealogy. The links in the chains are the ordinances of baptism, endowments, and sealings. These ordinances, performed in the temples by the living for the dead, are the welding of the links.

As I approached the place where I had entered, my attention was attracted to a small group of women preparing what appeared to be apparel. Observing my inquiring countenance, one of the women said they were preparing to receive a friend of mine, Brother Phillip Worthington. He died two days after my experience in the spirit world. I spoke at his funeral.

As I gasped his name, I was told that if I knew the joy and glorious mission that awaited him, I would not want to ask that he be detained longer on earth.

Then, flooding through my consciousness came the truth that the will of the Lord can be done on earth as it is in heaven only when we resign completely to his will and let his will be done in innocence and peace.

Men, women, and children are often called to missions of great importance on the other side. Some respond gladly, while others refuse to go, or their loved ones will not give them up. Also, many die because they have not faith to be healed. Yet others live long and pass out of this world of mortality without any special manifestations or actions of the divine will.

When a man, woman, or child is stricken ill, the prime importance is not if he is going to live or die. What matters whether he lives or dies, so long as the Father's will be done? Surely we can trust that person with God. Herein lies the special duty and privilege of administration by the priesthood. It is given the elders to divine the will of the Father concerning the one upon whose head their hands are laid. If, for any reason, they are unable to receive the Father's will, then they shall continue to pray in faith for the afflicted and humbly concede supremacy to the will of God, that his will be done on earth as it is in heaven.

Birth into the world of spirits is a glorious privilege and blessing. The greatest spirits in the family of the Father have not usually been permitted to tarry longer in the flesh than is necessary to perform a certain mission. They are called to the world of spirits, where the field is greater and the workers fewer.

Immediately, my body was quickened and I arose to ponder my experience and to declare to the world that—irrespective of what others may say or think—I do know of my own positive knowledge and from my own personal experience that Jesus Christ is the Son of the Father and the Savior of the world.

The spirit of man does not die, but survives the change called death and goes to the world of spirits, which is upon or near this world. Man's individuality is not lost in death, nor is his progress inhibited. The spirits will literally take up their bodies again in the resurrection. The principles of salvation are now being taught to the spirits and the great work of saving the Father's family among the living and the dead is in progress. Comparatively few will be lost. The gospel of Jesus Christ has again been established upon the earth with all the attendant keys, power, authority, and blessings through the Prophet Joseph Smith. This is not only the power that will save and exalt everyone who is obedient, but is also the power that will ultimately save the world. The burden of our mission is to save souls for God. The work for the living is no more important than the work for the dead who have passed beyond the veil.

"Everyone Had Something to Do"
by Heber Q. Hale
Copyright by CFI.
First published in *Beyond the Veil*
by Lee Nelson.

Treasure in the Graveyard

by Pat L. Sagers

My husband, Lynn, knows that because of my love for genealogical work I like old cemeteries. And I know that cemeteries have never interested him in the least.

Through the years, Lynn has been a good sport, however. He has learned to bring a book or a magazine when we travel so that when I find a cemetery I want to study, he can sit under a big shade tree and read while I hunt for names.

When we lived in Nephi, our house was only a couple of blocks from the cemetery. I had perused this graveyard so many times I thought I had memorized the locations of every one of my ancestors' graves. I was no longer really interested in the Nephi cemetery, but on a beautiful spring day in May 2001, my husband totally surprised me when he asked if I would like to take a walk down to the graveyard with him. This was something amazingly different. Of course I dropped what I was doing and said, "Yes!"

As we walked along, reading the names and inscriptions on the headstones, we came to a tiny white statue of a little girl sleeping on her side. It stood just a couple of rows from where my Fuller ancestors are buried. I had never really noticed this marker before. I pushed the grass back with my foot and called to Lynn, "Oh, this is a cute little headstone. But I can't read anything on it."

At once, Lynn came to look. I began to walk away from the headstone, but Lynn hurried to examine it. "Do you want me to see what it says?" he asked.

I didn't answer him. I had never seen him this curious

before—at least not in a cemetery. He got down on his hands and knees and pushed the grass away. "All it says is Electa," he told me.

A light suddenly turned on inside my head. "Lynn, my great-grandmother had a little girl who died, and her name was Electa."

When we got home, Lynn returned to his other projects. But I realized that now I had been nudged into motion. I decided to return to the cemetery. This time I took some clippers and a little digging shovel. When I cleared away the grass and dirt, I could tell that under her name was written, "Daughter of J. & A. Camborn." It was truly her grave! I was sure of it, even though the last name on the headstone had been misspelled "Camborn" instead of Cambron. The J. and A. indicated her parents, Joseph and Anne.

Since I had been the "family genealogist," and had access to the records, I looked through our family records on my Personal Ancestral File software. No one in our family knew the exact date or place where Electa had been buried. In fact, our family thought she had been buried in Eureka. The only story we had heard about Electa was that when she was six or seven years old, she woke up one night and asked for a drink of water. She was dead the next morning.

When I told Lynn what I had found on the headstone, and that I was positive this was our Electa, he again surprised me by suggesting that we get some cement and raise the headstone up so that at least her name could be read. So, helping me every step of the way, Lynn got some Quikrete mix, took a shovel, wheelbarrow, and hose, and dug up the headstone. To our surprise, we found more information! The complete headstone said: "ELECTA—daughter of J. & A. CAMBORN—died Nove. 1, 1886—Aged 6 Years—Gone, but not forgotten." And on the back of the headstone it read: "Sleep on dear child—And take thy rest."

I noticed that the headstone seemed a little out of place with the other headstones along that row, so I asked Lynn to dig more to the east. Sure enough, a couple of feet back, he found the original base of the headstone, with the front end broken off. We raised the base up, put the headstone back where it originally sat, and cemented it in place. Though the bottom part is discolored from sitting under the dirt for so many years—it must have broken off and someone had just propped it up in the dirt in the middle of her grave—everything on the headstone could be read.

After this experience, Lynn seemed more interested in cemeteries than I ever dreamed he would be. On Memorial Day, he went to Salt Lake City with me to decorate his mother's grave. I felt lucky for this, so when he didn't want to go with me to the Nephi graveyard when we got home, I didn't mind. When I slipped away to place some fresh flowers on the graves of my loved ones, my eyes searched first of all for the special gravestone we had carefully repaired. To my surprise, already lying across Electa's grave was one little live flower. Someone else had put a flower on her grave!

I couldn't imagine who would have put it there. The headstone had been buried for many, many years. As far as I knew, I was the only relative living there in Nephi.

There was joy in my heart as I left the graveyard that day. I didn't know who had left the flower on Electa's grave, but I left several more flowers, feeling grateful that we had been able to play a small part in making sure our little relative would never be forgotten.

Finding the treasure of Electa's grave had not only brought happiness to an unknown person, but it had been an opportunity for my amazing husband and me to find new appreciation for one another. I may not always see him as interested as this in the future, but this was an astounding and memorable time we spent on a precious little girl's grave, a time that brought us all closer together—Joseph, Anne, Electa, Lynn, and me.

My International Family

by John A. Harris

*J*ust weeks after I was baptized at the age of sixteen, my branch president called me to attend a family history class. Because of that simple assignment, my entire life changed.

Growing up in Uruguay with the uncommon surname of Harris (inherited from my father, who was British), I already had a natural interest in family history because of my unique ancestry—which includes progenitors from Switzerland and China, as well as Great Britain. The class made the Spirit of Elijah burn more brightly within me. I began to interview my grandparents, to fill in family group records, to complete pedigree charts, and to write my family history. Soon after completing the class, I was called to serve as a family history instructor.

During the next few years, I experienced spiritual direction several times while working on my family history, and since then I have learned that events like these are common when we are engaged in this great work.

Archived Records in Uruguay

One of my most extraordinary experiences took place when I was nineteen years old. I was released from serving as a counselor in my branch presidency so I could accept an assignment as chairman of family history for the mission. We were preparing for a visit from George H. Fudge of the Church's Genealogical Department in Salt Lake City; he was hoping to microfilm some of the vital records in Uruguay. I was asked to help make the arrangements.

That night I prayed fervently for the ability to do what I had been asked. Later I noticed a newspaper headline that read, "Genealogy in Uruguay." The story told about an upcoming meeting of Uruguayan genealogists. Then I saw that the newspaper was several days old. The meeting had already been held, but I decided to visit the address in the story anyway.

On the evening I decided to make my visit, I was also assigned to supervise a youth gathering, and I had to stay at the meetinghouse until 9:30 P.M. I didn't have the money for bus fare, so I walked to the place where the meeting had been held. By the time I reached the address, it was late. I rang the bell, hoping for the best. A few minutes later, a man opened the door.

I introduced myself, and the man graciously allowed me to come in. What he said next filled me with surprise: "I am glad you came this late because I just arrived. Had you come a few minutes earlier, you would have found an empty house." I soon learned that he was part of the only group of genealogists in Uruguay. I also found out that the newspaper had published the story about the meeting despite having been asked not to do so.

I was able to set up a meeting for Brother Fudge with this group of eminent genealogists. They opened the archives to him. At his request, some of the indexes of family history records in Uruguay were microfilmed. I believe that these were the first records microfilmed by the Church in Uruguay.

A Chinese Poem of Generations

A second significant event occurred a few years later when I was called to serve a mission to Peru. My grandfather, who was not religious but was the man I respected most, did not want me to go. Mine was a Chinese family, and my grandfather was its patriarch. In effect, the family was our religion, and obeying and honoring our elders was our moral code. For weeks my grandfather did not talk to me because of my intention to go on a mission. One week before I left, he offered me a present. He gave me the razor I was to use during my mission—a razor I still keep to this day. He was a loving man. In order to help him feel better about my mission, I told him I would do what I could to find his relatives living in Peru.

In the first three months of my mission, I met Guillermo "Willy" Hauyon, my grandfather's nephew. I told Guillermo that I had heard there was a Chinese poem in the family from which each generation took a word and incorporated it into their given names. To my surprise, he produced the poem and copied it for me. When I returned to Uruguay after my mission, I had my grandfather transcribe the poem in his own handwriting. Today it is a precious reminder of my grandfather and my heritage. The poem contains forty-eight Chinese characters and is used to mark generations. It has since proven invaluable in helping determine family relations.

A few months after finding the poem—while serving in the mission office—I traveled to Trujillo, Peru. There I met Elsa Hauyon, who was then eighty-two years old. She turned out to be my grandfather's cousin, the only relative I have ever known who grew up with him in China. I spent hours talking to her, recording the names of my grandfather's brothers and sisters. I learned that there were thirteen of them, not just the four my grandfather spoke of. With Elsa's help, I also traced our family back to the founder of my grandfather's hometown.

Swiss Ancestors in Peru

Another sacred family history event also occurred while I served as a missionary. Upon arriving in Peru, I was assigned to Callao, the port of Lima. It was most remarkable because, unbeknownst to me at the time, the tombs of my Swiss ancestors were in that city. A relative eventually told me about the tombs, but I was unable to find them before being transferred to another city.

However, I believe that the Lord wanted me to find my ancestors. While missionaries are seldom assigned to the same branch twice, I was. Almost a year later, I came back to Callao, and this time I discovered there were two adjacent cemeteries—one where my Schlupp ancestors are buried and the other where the records (dating back to 1820) for the family are stored. Searching through the records, I finally came across what I was looking for: "Elizabeth Schlupp, fifty-seven years old, buried September 16, 1875; Ana Maria Schlupp Kruse, sixty-six years old, buried January 24, 1918." I had found my Swiss ancestors!

I was ecstatic. I was able to complete four generations of my family history at last. Of all the places I could have been assigned, the Lord had called me not once but twice to Callao—the place where I could locate my Swiss ancestors.

A Lasting Impression

All of these wonderful events happened during the six years after my baptism. When I look back on my youth, I realize how much my testimony of the Church and its divinity has been strengthened through family history work and the Spirit of Elijah. I can truly say I have felt the Lord's influence many times in turning my heart to my ancestors. That chord, struck by my branch president, who was inspired to get me started at age sixteen with family history, still resonates today in the most sacred experiences of my soul.

"My First Church Assignment," by
John A. Harris, Area Authority Seventy.
First published in the *Ensign*, August 2003.

Standing with Our People

by Gary Hannig

We all agree that prayer is a mighty connection with the heavens. But so is the astonishing power of reaching out to those men and women through the ages who gave us our bodies, our lives. To find their names and, if we are lucky, their faces in an old photograph, and to know that they love us and are probably standing near us at times, often waiting for us to perform their ordinances—what an overwhelming spiritual experience.

When I found the story my mother had written about my grandmother, I felt that powerful connection. As a young bride, Julia had come with her husband Alf Syphus to the rough mining town of St. Thomas; because of my mother's story, I could share Julia's experiences when I read how they lived. Alf had a contract to carry mail from St. Thomas to the mining towns along the Colorado River, and it was necessary for him to be away from home every other night. Because the town was infested with out-laws and desperadoes, Uncle Alf built a platform high up in a cottonwood tree that stood near their small adobe cabin. On the nights he was away, my grandmother Julia would make her bed in the tree and pull the long ladder up beside her. Then she would lie in terror as the desperadoes went through the streets on their drunken sprees, shooting their guns and cursing. I could sympa-thize with her frightening experience.

Perhaps my assurance that our ancestors are truly stand-ing close by comes from another amazing experience—this one involving my mother, the youngest child of Grandmother Julia's second marriage, to Luke Whitney. Because she was the youngest, as a teenager she sometimes stayed alone while Julia and Luke went to their nearby ranch to harvest crops. Feeling lonely one evening, she decided to walk out to meet them. She walked past Gibson's vineyard, the school, and the tree where her mother had slept many years before. She turned the corner where Jacob Bauer's blacksmith shop had stood, and walked across the small Muddy River bridge, not far from the larger destroyed bridge across the Virgin River, which had burned so badly no one could cross on it, though its metal underpinnings still stood bare and scarred against the sky. She wrote:

> A bright moon was rising and the desert seemed warm and friendly, so I went on, thinking I would soon hear the sound of the horse-drawn wagon of my parents, who were probably on their way home to get me. But I did not hear them when I reached the summit of the foothills, nor when I was walking down the steep dugways on the other side.
>
> A short distance from the Virgin Ford was a sand hill. It was a warm autumn night, and I sat with my chin on my knees, dreaming young-woman dreams and reminiscing as I listened to the wind in the chaparral bushes. Then I realized it was not the wind in the chaparral I was listening to, but a choir—a beautiful choir. I could distinctly hear the soprano, the tenor, the bass, the rich alto. I could hear the mighty crescendos, the beautiful harmony of sound coming from the river channel beyond the burned bridge. At first I thought it must be my imagination, but as I listened, I knew that I was actually listening to a choir.
>
> Suddenly, I grew afraid. I knew that by no earthly means could the singing come to me. A radio never entered my mind, for they were not in common use at that time, and the only one in town was used with earphones.
>
> I don't know how long I sat there feeling helpless and fearful. I realized that it was late now, and my parents had probably decided to stay at the ranch on

this night. I knew that somehow I would have to get back to town alone. When I found strength to get to my feet, my impulse was to run, but reason told me I would be exhausted before reaching the summit of the hills. By sheer willpower I made myself walk up the dugways. With all my heart I wished someone were with me. Even the howl of a coyote or the shadowy outline of a desert fox would have been welcome.

As I crossed the summit, I breathed a hesitant sigh of relief. And when I was out of the hills and could see the dim light of the coal-oil lamps in a few windows, my fear was gone. As I entered my town, although the streets were empty, I could feel its warmth and friendliness shielding me from harm. I paused a moment beside my mother's "bedroom tree" and remembered that she had been afraid in its branches. I had probably felt the same fear. I also believed I knew what Luke was writing about in the scriptures when the shepherds on the Judean hills "were sore afraid."

As I lay alone that night I could not stop thinking about the marvelous music I had heard. After the fear left me, a marvelous faith and hope warmed my heart. I knew I could not tell anyone of this experience, for I would be ridiculed. Of course my father and mother would understand. Papa would hold my hand in his rough, calloused one, and quote a bit of scripture or poetry. And a special glow would light Mama's beautiful eyes and face.

As the government began to build the Hoover Dam, which would cover our town with water, and as the modern miracles of movies, satellites, and interplanetary travel began to take place, our lives changed. As I grew older and had my own family, and as we began observing these great modern developments, one day I decided to tell a special friend of my own faith the story of my experience hearing the choir music.

She was a dear friend, and she looked at me with

a smile. "Was there any kind of metal near you?" she asked.

Simultaneously I remembered two things—the steel spans of the old burned bridge, and a story I had read of a train wreck in the early history of the West: how a man far away had heard a voice coming from the metal bedstead in his room, and learned of the wreck in that way. Although it was long before the invention of the radio, the same principles were involved.

I do not know how the sound of this choir came to me. But after this experience, I began to imagine that someday through some undreamed-of modern technology, we may hear many more of the sounds of the universe. My thought was that, of course, it is possible that someday our technology could enable us to pick up the sounds of our loved ones who have left their words and music circling in the sky. I know that some of today's technology—television, computers, space travel—were undreamed-of miracles in my day. I knew that miracles have always happened. And I knew I had heard one that night.

This story of my mother's is precious to our family. Since she wrote it, I have seen excerpts on television of technological advances that have picked up—though still crudely—sound impulses and voices from the past that are still circling in the air. The idea that we are still living with not only their spirits but also the voices of our loved ones surrounding us gives us even more motivation to tune in and listen to what they want to tell us.

Because my dear mother was an avid genealogist, I have always felt that I should continue her work so that it would not be in vain. When I finally retired and had the time, I took a twelve-week course in family history training with my wife and began to put together pedigree charts, family records, and life stories—to build a CD I could give my family for a Christmas present. Like a miracle, the way opened up for me.

One day, at a meeting in a neighboring stake building, I

happened to find a brochure giving the phone number of a "Land and Records Office" in Nauvoo. Since I have ancestors that were converted to the Church in its early days and settled Far West, Missouri, and Nauvoo, Illinois, and we had planned to visit Nauvoo, I thought that it would be an amazing experience if I could find the exact spot where my ancestors had built their home. So I called the Land and Records office to ask if they could give me any information.

I was thrilled with their response. Within two weeks I received a computer disk in the mail; to my amazement, it contained not only a plat map of the city with the property that my forebearers owned, but several pages of information that—though I believed my mother had already done all of the research—I realized I did not have. There were records not only of the living ordinances that my ancestors had performed in the Nauvoo Temple just prior to their being driven out of Nauvoo in 1846, but records of work for the dead that had been done, including baptisms that had been done as far back as 1841. It listed who the proxies were that performed that work; it listed the ordination of one of my ancestors to the office of Seventy and the person who ordained him. It even reported that my ancestor—James William Huntsman—was one of the signers of the Missouri Petitions.

I was so grateful. I felt a connection not only to my ancestors, but to those who had gone before me to research all of this information. If I had been an experienced genealogist, I may have been able to uncover this information for myself. How remarkable it seemed to me that someone had already done all that work, and that it came so readily in such a short period of time.

As I give my carefully prepared Christmas gifts this year to my children and their children, I pray that their hearts will turn to their fathers, as mine is turning to them. I so much want for all of us to be together in the house of the Lord, to experience joy as we join all of the thousands and thousands of people who have gone before us and whose voices we may not only someday hear on this earth, but also in our visits with those wonderful people beyond the grave. If we broaden our sense of relationships, we will include all of heaven's inhabitants and all of mankind, and love them as our own.

One of my four sons is adopted into our family, and another of my sons and his wife recently adopted a little girl from China. At the sealing in the Manti Temple, the tears ran down our faces as we realized that our oldest son and this little girl are as much a part of us as though we had given birth to them.

We are in a world where we must learn to love everyone. We want the best for every person on earth, and we want to make a vow to teach them, to protect them, to give our time for them, and to give our lives for them if need be, just as those of our military are doing, so that the ideology of the gospel may reign supreme—so that the countries will open up to allow the millennium to be ushered in, that we may become a sanctified world. This is what our heavenly parents want for us—and why the Savior made the sacrifice of the AT-ONE-MENT—so that we would become one.

My Grandmother's Cookbook

by Cheryl C. Huff

*P*erhaps our family believed that they needed a lot of help from each other to prepare good meals. Or they were all such excellent cooks they just wanted to share recipes. Whatever the reason, many years ago, the members of the family got together and printed a family cookbook.

By the time I was a cook, all of the volumes were out of commission or missing. I had my own modern cookbook, and though I had heard about the great family masterpiece, I had traded my interest in cooking for other interests, especially genealogy.

The love of genealogical research in my life came when I was first converted to the Church and the mother of one of my friends took me to the Family History Library in Salt Lake City. I spent most of that first day finding nothing and feeling discouraged. Then, just as I had made up my mind that I was never going to do this again, and I was ready to catch our bus to return home, a woman tapped me on the shoulder and said that I looked frustrated. She wanted to know if she could help me.

When I told her that we were just leaving and I didn't think I wanted to come here anymore, she asked to see what name I was researching. She told me to follow her, and within minutes she had found my ancestor on the 1850 Census.

I had just looked at that same census a few hours before, but had found the writing to be faint and unreadable. This time my entry was the second one on the film, and I could read it clearly. From that moment on, I was hooked.

There was one line I had been working on, however, that

seemed to take me forever. When I was researching the Preston family, I finally felt that I had all of the children identified and I was in the process of having the temple work done for them, when I had a chance to travel to Southern California to visit my mother.

While I was there, my mother had been busy cleaning out closets, and had come across the old family cookbook. She recognized it as one her mother had used. When she came back, she had it in her hands. Because it had belonged to my grandmother, she thought I would like to have it. "You can have this, Cheryl," she told me. "This is the famous cookbook put together by our family members years ago. This one belonged to your grandmother. You might find something useful in it."

At first when I took the book from her, I thought perhaps she was making a slur against my cooking. But I didn't put up any fuss. I simply told her thank you and took it, glad to have something that had been so valuable to my grandmother.

When I looked inside the cover of the book, however, I was amazed. There was the entire genealogy for the Preston family of Lewis Cass Preston and Sarah Corson, and more.

On this list were two other entries. They were for two unnamed baby girls who had died at birth. I could not believe it. I had never been told about these little girls. I was excited to find them, though I was afraid it might not be true. However, I found a confirmation that these two babies had both been born and had lived for a short time.

I was so delighted to have these little girls identified and listed with their other siblings that the cookbook became a treasure to me. I was especially thrilled to have these babies sealed to their parents. I was so grateful for the family cookbook and how it has blessed several generations in different ways.

Finding Grandpa Pablo

by Raquel Pedraza de Brosio

*M*y father was born in the Chaco region in northeastern Argentina, where the sun is hot and people work the soil, growing cotton and other crops. Neighbors have known each other for generations, and traditions are followed to the letter. My father's family lived in Villa Angela, where they had a comfortable, middle-class life.

Then, when my father was nine years old, his parents separated, and my father went with his mother and sisters to live in Buenos Aires. This was quite a difficult change for a young boy who couldn't understand why he had to leave his hometown and his friends, and who didn't know when he would see his father again. As the months of separation turned into years, my father's memory of his own father faded. He didn't even have a photograph of him.

Our family was introduced to the restored gospel and eventually joined the Church. When I was fifteen, I became quite interested in family history work. Seeking out my ancestors became a passion with me, and I was able to become well acquainted with my family on my mother's side. But on my father's side, all of my attempts ended with one name: Grandpa Pablo Pedraza.

When my father told me the story of his childhood, I had a strong desire to find out more about Grandpa Pablo. We began to pray as a family to find out more about him so we could complete our family history. My father probed his memory, and he managed to recall the address of an elderly aunt. He wrote to her, but she had passed away before we were able to get the information we were seeking. We didn't give up; we continued to pray.

One day on my father's way to work, the bus he was riding stopped at a traffic light beside a mail truck. My father could see several large packages in the truck, and one drew his attention. On its label was the name Pablo Pedraza, and it gave an address in my father's childhood hometown.

Quite excitedly, my father wrote down the address. He knew that his father had been an auto mechanic, and he thought that the large box on the truck could easily have been for him. For several years we wrote to this address, expressing our hope that we had found our father and grandfather, and saying that we had a desire to meet with him. But we never received an answer.

One day, my father was telling this story to a friend in our ward. The friend suggested, "Why don't you just go there and find him?" Fear flooded our minds. Maybe Grandpa Pablo did not want us to find him, or maybe this was not his address.

After praying about it, we felt that we needed to travel to Chaco to look for Grandpa Pablo. Our whole family loaded into the van and drove for twenty-eight hours. Driving straight to the address on the package, we stopped in front of a pretty, well-kept house. A man of about sixty was outside, washing his car. My father gathered his courage and got out to introduce himself and verify that we were on the right street.

Our family watched expectantly through the van windows. After several minutes, we saw our father and the man exchange a big hug. They both began to motion for us to get out of the van. It was indeed Grandpa Pablo—the father my father had not seen for forty years!

The meeting was not an easy one, but a spirit of love was there. We learned that because of the inadequate postal service in his small hometown, Grandpa Pablo had not received any of the letters we had sent him over the years. We also learned that he had tried to find my father for many years, but that he had his own fears about meeting us. We met Grandpa's wife and children and learned about their joys and sorrows. We learned that Grandpa Pablo was a good man who believed in God. He was a loving husband and father and a good neighbor. And we could see that he was as excited to get to know us as we were to finally find him.

Now we have photographs of Grandpa Pablo and vital information about him and some of his ancestors. He died one year ago, and we are preparing to go to the temple to do ordinance work for him and other family members. My father can hardly contain this joy that he will finally be able to be sealed to his parents. The work on our family history chart continues.

We have been promised that "the heart of the fathers [shall turn] to the children, and the heart of the children to their fathers" (Malachi 4:6). Our family was greatly blessed to have the Lord lead us by the hand so that this promise could literally be fulfilled.

A Great Missionary

by Jeanne Davey

I often visited my uncle, Ralph Davey, and his wife, Beth Snelgrove Davey (yes, she was related to the ice cream mogul) before they passed away quite a few years ago. They said they had planned on leaving this frail existence at the age of about eighty-eight, and they were now in their mid-nineties. I came to cheer them up and give them courage through these last few years when they thought they had already done their life's work. They weren't quite sure what was left for them. I didn't believe there was any purpose to my visits other than for me to offer love and hope, until during one of the last times I was in their home I found something that seemed to be important to them—and to me.

On one particular day, when I was on my way out the door, I happened to glance down at an old photograph on a table beside a chair. The image looked ancient—the faded portrait of an austere gentleman.

"Who is this?" I asked my uncle.

"Oh, that is our many times great-grandfather Isaac Russell."

I had never heard of Isaac Russell. What Ralph told me is that he was one of the first eight missionaries to visit Great Britain. He also told me the story of his conversion.

Both John Taylor and Isaac Russell had been conducting their own Sunday services in Toronto, Canada, when an enthusiastic young man by the name of Parley P. Pratt had come to talk to the congregation. John Taylor was rather cold toward Pratt.

He remained uninterested in what he had to say. However, in his congregation was Mary Russell, a sister of Isaac. Mary was very interested in what Parley P. Pratt had to say. Immediately she invited Parley to preach in their home, and their family listened intently to the gospel of the Restoration.

I was fascinated by Ralph's story and wanted to take the old photograph of Isaac Russell to BYU. Ralph was happy to send it with me, knowing the skill of the university in preparing and restoring old photographs. But this valuable piece wasn't even a photograph. It was such an early image that it was done on glass. In order to see it, the viewer had to put an opaque surface behind it.

"Where did you get this?" the expert wanted to know.

After I told him that my aunt and uncle had kept it all these years, and that I had been instructed that it had been taken in 1838, he shook his head.

"This kind of photographic process had not yet come to this continent in 1838."

Puzzling for a moment, I realized what had happened. "Was it done in Great Britain?" I asked.

"Yes," he said slowly.

"Then he had this photograph made when he was on his mission to England."

That was the answer. This wonderful old photograph of Isaac Russell had been made in England when he and John Taylor and all of the other pioneering missionaries had sailed to the British Isles.

My brother, Bruce Davey, was thrilled with the story of the old image on glass. In his hometown of Bellevue, Washington, he gave a speech in which he told the story of the old photograph and the honor that Isaac Russell had brought to the Davey family through his service as one of the first eight missionaries to the British Isles.

After his speech, a woman came up to him. With bright eyes, she said, "I am descended from that Russell line."

This was exciting news to my brother. Through this connection, we were able to go back through the Russells who had come to America. They were metallurgists and miners. We then found that the lines went all the way back to Prussia. We discovered that our Prussian ancestors spelled the name "Rossel," and had changed it to "Russell" only when they came to England and eventually Canada, looking for mining opportunities.

My Russell line eventually became "Davey" and married into the Cannon line. The maiden name of one of President George Q. Cannon's wives was "Davey." When the federal government came and threatened to break up the polygamous families, to be safe, she had to keep her maiden name. How special it was to discover my connection to this great missionary.

Temple Ready

by Elder B. Markham

*D*uring the war in West Africa, when so many lost their lives, the Liberian members of the LDS Church were grateful that their Monrovia stake building had survived.

When they were asked to put in a Family History Center, they were enthusiastic and willing to do whatever the Church authorities required of them. They had the space and the motivation. However, most of them had little or no experience with computers. And there were no computers or software programs in their Family History Center.

When the temple came to Ghana, these Liberians were so happy. After they had seen their prophet, Gordon B. Hinckley, and experienced the temple dedication, a large group of them wanted nothing more than to do ordinance work in the temple. They read the instructions carefully. In order for them to perform temple work for their dead, they must make all of the names of their ancestors "temple ready" by putting them on computer disks.

Fifty-eight Liberians began to prepare to make the journey to the temple. Hoping to accomplish the task they had set out to do, many of the members saved their money for weeks, taking out a few pennies here and there from their meager wages to prepare for their temple project. The most inexpensive way to get their names on disks was to buy old, used disks. However, it was still expensive to pay someone who knew about computers to write their material on the disks. Desiring to be completely obedient, they handwrote what family genealogy information they had and then paid to have the information either typed into a word processing program or scanned as a picture file. When their information had been digitized, they had their records stored on the disks.

When it was time to go to the temple, the Liberians carefully wrapped each disk in a sheet of paper to keep it clean. These disks (about twenty) were carried together in a plastic grocery bag and presented at the temple as "temple ready computer disks." They were not. But who could be critical of such an effort? The Liberians gave the bag of disks to the missionaries.

Sister Armstrong and Sister Markham exchanged guarded looks. There were hours of work that would need to be done with these disks if they were to be ready for use in the near future. They knew the Liberians could not stay long; they needed to return to their homes and jobs, meager as they might be.

The missionaries began to get to work. They will not say how long they stayed at their computers to get all of the information they could off the disks. But they knew this was why they came to the mission field. It was a work they loved. Elder Armstrong then entered the available names into Personal Ancestral File software. Disks that couldn't be read were assigned to Elder Markham, who downloaded recovery software from the Internet and recovered much of the data.

The team effort paid off. By Wednesday, all of the information the Liberians had brought was safely stored in PAF files. The Armstrongs spent three days working with each member to fill in blanks and gather extra names, dates, and places.

Although statistics aren't as important as the joy these people felt in being able to perform temple work for their loved ones, it is interesting to note that since the Accra Ghana Temple was dedicated in January of 2004, the most ordinances done during a single week were done the week of March 1, 2005, when the fifty-eight Liberians were there.

Research with Spirit

by John L. Hart

*S*piritual guidance is essential in family history research, said David E. Rencher, director of the Libraries Division of the Family History Department of the LDS Church.

"All of my research skills don't compensate for what goes on on the other side of the veil—that's the only way to explain it," he told a gathering at the annual BYU Family History Fireside, held at the Wilkinson Student Center on November 12, 2004.

He explained that "while I have adequate genealogical skills, and while I try to use those, there are times when, no matter how good my skills, I could not connect to the sources."

Once, he said, he had a "haunting feeling that one daughter was missing" in a family. He happened to visit friends in the East who were aware of his interest in family history research.

"I do have an unusual surname, and she remembered it," he said. A few months after the visit, he received a note from one of the friends whose job was to receive donations to the Annandale Public Library in Virginia. A family Bible had been donated, and "the surname is Rencher," he said. "It contained the entry I had been looking for."

Abraham Rencher was a five-term congressman, and it turned out that one of his daughters had been taken with scarlet fever, died in Washington, D.C., and was not buried with the rest of the family.

"How many public libraries are there in Virginia or the United States? Is it a coincidence that the person who goes through gift boxes in Annandale Virginia is the one person who knows me? . . .

I would submit that councils are held on the other side of the veil in this important work," he said.

He told of not being able to find any source material on a family for whom he was searching until he traveled to Atlanta, Georgia, for a conference. He went a few days early and stayed in Montgomery, Alabama, in order to visit a cemetery near the place he thought this family had once lived.

"One of the things I have noted frequently is that the promptings of the Spirit are not only very subtle, but very pleading," he said. "While some can be very strong, others are just very brief."

Such a brief prompting came during this trip.

"The Jazz basketball team was doing exceptionally well in the play-offs, and when I checked into my hotel . . . and turned on the TV, the game had just started." As he held the remote and contemplated what he should do, "I was impressed to put the remote down," he said.

"I headed for a cemetery and on the way passed another cemetery near where I was headed. Being a good genealogist, no way could I pass that cemetery and go on down the road."

In this cemetery he found the grave of a family member he hadn't known about, and while he was there a noisy, speeding pickup truck passed and skidded to a halt. A man climbed out. This man took him to the cemetery he'd started out to visit—where he found the graves of the family for whom he was searching. Then this stranger introduced him to relatives living nearby, who introduced him to other relatives, took him to the family homestead, gave him copies of their family history and pictures, and invited him to family reunions.

"There, in a couple of days, the wealth of material that came . . . was overwhelming. I think, many times, of how I stood there with the remote in hand. Had I not gone that very moment, I would not have been in the cemetery when the truck drove by. Instead, I would have been in Montgomery, Alabama, watching the Jazz lose a play-off game."

He told of an associate who took a temple trip from Oregon to the Oakland Temple. During free time afterward, he headed to the Family History Library. Another member noticed and asked if he could accompany him.

"My friend admits that he was crestfallen," said Brother Rencher, explaining that he didn't want to spend his valuable research time helping a beginner. But he took the man along, and as they entered the library, he pointed to one of three women at the reference desk. "Tell her what you want to find, and she will help you," he said, and then disappeared in the library's aisles to do his own research.

"So he walked over to the woman and said, 'I really don't know why I am here. I don't know what I am going to work on.'"

She asked what he knew about his family and he responded, "Well, we have a family tradition that my second great-grandfather rode into a town [in Nebraska] on an old white plow horse at about age ten and would never, never talk about where he came from."

She replied, "We have a family tradition in our family that when he was ten years old, our second great uncle took the old white plow horse and was never seen again."

Brother Rencher said, "My friend found absolutely nothing in the library, which was poetic justice, but this man and this woman indeed were cousins; they had extended that line considerably and it was a great find for him."

He emphasized, "We cannot overcome the promptings of the Spirit and expect to find what we are looking for. We must not build systems in today's age that take the Spirit out of this work."

"I love my computer," he said. "I love it for everything it can do, but . . . the computer is not what turned my heart. What turns my heart are the experiences and impressions I have from the Spirit, and the things I know and understand."

He finally observed that the words of Malachi stating that Elijah the prophet shall "turn the heart of the fathers to the children, and the heart of the children to their fathers" (Malachi 4:5-6) appear in all four of the standard works. He said, "As we do this work, we do perfect the Saints and we do missionary work on the other side. And those who are prepared and those who are ready to receive the blessings of the gospel, I think, see to it that events are orchestrated and things come into play. And if we will listen to those promptings—and sometimes they are very slight—the Spirit will lead us."

"And Someday, We Will Meet These People"
by John D. Hart. Reprinted by permission of the
"Church News" section of the *Deseret Morning
News*, November 20, 2004.

Documents Meant To Be Saved

by Ruth Martinson

*M*y friend Delana Youmans, who lived on an air force base in Alaska with her husband, told me that a woman on that base had a meaningful experience. The woman—whose name we'll say is Katherine—told this story in a stake conference talk one Sunday in Alaska, and Sister Youmans never forgot it.

For a long time, Katherine had been working on her genealogy, and at last she had received some priceless family documents from a relative in the South. Excited about receiving these documents, she had placed them carefully in what she believed was the safest place in the house—with her silverware in a buffet drawer.

It was not long afterward that she became ill and had to go to the hospital for a short time. Her oldest daughter, who was sixteen, assured her mother that she could take care of the four younger children while their father was on duty. One morning, this daughter was tending the four younger children when they suddenly heard a terrible noise. It was one of the planes coming in for a crash landing.

When the plane finally landed, it went through three houses. As it plowed through Sister Youman's house, which held the children, an explosion caught the house on fire. Terrified, the sixteen-year-old daughter gathered up the children and crawled out of a window before they could save anything in the house. The children watched as the entire structure went up in flames.

Feeling grateful that their lives were saved, the children watched their home burn to the ground. They were heartsick to see that their neighbor's house—the third house the plane had torn apart—was not only burning, but had been crushed like matchsticks to the ground. Later they learned that the man who had been living in this house had been killed.

As they watched the destruction, they did not know about the precious family documents their mother had received and placed in the drawer of the buffet.

When the mother got out of the hospital, concerned and heartsick, she took the children with her to sift through the ashes of the house to discover if anything at all had been preserved. As she looked in the blackened area of what had once been the dining room, she found that the silverware had all been melted into blackened puddles and solid knots.

However, the mother saw a folder under the damaged silverware box that she thought she recognized. Hurriedly, she pulled the folder out of the ashes. She could not believe her eyes. The priceless documents had been preserved! It was unimaginable to her. The tears began to run down her cheeks. She could not believe what had happened, except to know with more certainty than ever that she must continue her efforts for her relatives, who were surely waiting for her to perform the work that they were praying would be done.

When I was working in Willard's Convalescent Home in Provo, Utah, on the night shift from about 1973 to 1977, a young girl worked with me for a time, and we would often talk to each other when we weren't busy. One night, she told me the very same story that Delana Youmans had told me so many years ago about this woman in Alaska finding that her priceless genealogical records had been preserved from a fire by a miracle. Startled, I looked at this young woman and told her that I had heard this story before from a friend of mine. This time, she assured me, I was hearing it from someone who was an eyewitness. For she herself was the young woman who had been sixteen years old and had saved the children and had seen her mother's joy when she found the documents.

That was thirty years ago, but I was so impressed that I have never forgotten this story.

The Potter's Signature

by Jean Marshall

*B*ack in 1981, a signature on the bottom of a beautiful piece of pottery in Ireland prompted me to write to the potter and inquire about his family history. It was a long shot because I appeared to be at a dead end in my family research. I was surprised not only to receive the most delightful reply, but a bouquet as well.

Our family was living in London for six months while my husband directed a group of forty college students in a study abroad program. With limited experience in doing family history research, I had—before I left the States—contacted my mother's cousin, who was an expert genealogist. She gave me some invaluable material, and I asked what I might do for her in return while we were in London. So she gave me a list of names to research— for dates of birth, death, and/or marriage certificates. In addition to performing this task, I decided to set myself the goal of finding the parents of my mother's ancestor Elizabeth Wolstenholme, who was born in 1755 in Sheffield, England. Her parents were not listed in the genealogical information I had.

Armed with these two goals, I began the research in earnest. I decided to look up Elizabeth Wolstenholme first, but I soon learned at the Hyde Park Family History Center that there are thousands, or at least hundreds, of Wolstenholmes of various spellings. I looked through many of them, but could not find one with the right dates. Discouraged, I set that project aside.

I managed to find quite a few dates for my cousin's list of names. But I still felt bothered that there was no Elizabeth

Wolstenholme, and I felt that I did not want to leave London without finding her and knowing something about her parents.

Near the end of our stay, we took the students on a bus trip in Ireland. One rainy day, the bus stopped for a few hours in Killarney. Some of us stepped into a wonderful shop of local handicrafts. We admired the handwoven shawls, knitted sweaters, and other beautiful gifts. I was immediately attracted to a display of handsome pottery. Admiring one bowl, I turned it over and read the signature scratched into the clay. It read "Peter Wolstenholme."

When I put the bowl back onto the counter, I thought of the vast number of names I had found at the Family History Center. I said to myself, "Peter Wolstenholme. Well, you certainly have a common name in England."

However, after returning to London, I could not stop thinking about that signature. So I wrote to Peter Wolstenholme's studio in Ireland and inquired if this Peter W. happened to know much about his family history, and if, by chance, there was in his family tree an Elizabeth born in 1755 who married a Peter Totley.

To my surprise, I received a prompt reply and a beautifully drawn bouquet of flowers! Peter Wolstenholme had sketched the bouquet of flowers and written, "Congratulations! You've done it! We appear to be gt. gt. gt. gt. gt. cousins!"

With his clever pen, he had also diagramed the progeny of Thomas and Grace Wolstenholme, their eight children, including twins—Anthony and Elizabeth—and Peter's own son, John.

He then added his father's name and address and told me that if I would write to him, he could help me. His father wrote immediately, sending me a handwritten copy of an extended family tree, carefully drawn on four sheets of paper all taped together to make a huge chart. Dozens of names and significant information augmented my mother's line.

I am convinced that when we commit to this research and make a serious effort, unexpected avenues open up to us. It brings to mind Goethe's observation: "Until one is committed there is hesitancy, the chance to draw back, always ineffectiveness.

Concerning all acts of existence and creation, there is one elementary truth, the ignorance of which kills countless ideas and splendid plans; that the moment one definitely commits oneself, then providence moves, too. All sorts of things occur to help one that would never otherwise have occurred. A whole stream of events issues from the decision, raising in one's favor all manner of unforeseen incidents and meetings and material assistance, which no man could have dreamt would have come his way."

I Felt Her Joy

by Darla Isackson

*M*y story actually begins with an inspired calling that continues to bring wonderful blessings to our family. Six years ago, my husband, Doug, and I were called to be family history consultants in our ward. Doug is the only person I know personally who has received that calling before attending the temple. Doug was a new convert when we began the challenging adventure of living as a blended family. My expectation was that he would quickly progress in the gospel and go to the temple. As the years passed, however, I became discouraged.

Swimming Upstream

For most of my life, I had dabbled in family history work. I knew the importance of it. However, in the crush of responsibilities with our large combined family and a full-time job, I had made no recent progress except for helping my mother complete her picture history. When I mentioned family history, she seemed to have no interest at all.

After we received this calling—which Doug willingly accepted—we realized we had to be *doing* family history in order to help others. We quickly learned that Doug's great-grandmother Wendla on his mother's side had not had her work done, but we could find no documentation for her. Doug's mother said that she had no information that would help us, and his grandparents were all dead. Doug's only uncle had an old family Bible written in Finnish, and a hand-lettered pedigree chart that gave no more information than we already had about Wendla. The family were Swedes whose ancestors had immigrated to Finland. The great-grandparents had later immigrated to the U.S. His great grandmother Wendla's full name was recorded in two different ways, both different from the way his mother had always spelled it. How could we know which spelling was accurate? With our limited skills, we could find nothing on the computer for any of the spellings.

Breakthrough

One day, I was pondering a particular phrase in my patriarchal blessing about doing vicarious work for those who had gone before. The blessing mentioned that I would inspire and influence loved ones. My parents had been avid genealogists, even taking part in a family organization that paid for professional researchers. The work was done as far back as records were then available. I had always felt there was little that I, a novice, could possibly do to add to those efforts. Consequently, that phrase from my blessing had frustrated me.

However, on that day, the sweet voice of the Spirit told that me those loved ones mentioned in my blessing included my husband's family. For whatever reason, perhaps because we had not yet been sealed in the temple, that possibility had never occurred to me.

This strong validation not only gave me a great desire to facilitate family history and temple work for my husband's ancestors, but also gave me pause. If Doug's family were my loved ones, did that mean that before this life I somehow knew I would be in this second marriage? Had I known and loved these people in the premortal existence and promised to be a "savior on Mount Zion" in regard to their temple work? If so, how could I move ahead? We had so little information about this untouched line, and Doug and I were barely beginning to learn about research.

The very next week, Doug's mother called me and said that she had just found an envelope that her uncle's widow had sent her years ago. She wondered if the information might interest us.

Did it ever! The envelope contained certificates that documented the dates and places of Wendla's birth and death. It also gave her parents' names—which no one had previously known for sure. Now we knew the correct spelling of Wendla's name. The documents also contained information about both of Wendla's husbands: the great-grandfather who died before Doug was born, and his step-great-grandfather whom he remembers. Now we could do their work also.

I'd heard a lot of family stories about Wendla. She had a true shotgun wedding. Her father insisted on the marriage when her intended husband, learning she was pregnant, tried to abandon her. Word had it that she despised this man for running out on her, and she made life hard for him but wouldn't give him a divorce. He died ten years later of "miner's lung." Wendla was an anti-Mormon bootlegger in Salt Lake City during Prohibition days. She was still a drinker when she married Doug's step-great-grandfather years later. From all we could gather, she had little use for any kind of religion until her final years, when she suffered from a fatal disease and turned back to her Protestant roots. I honestly didn't have much faith that she was eager to have her work done.

My Surprise Joy

Doug and I prepared the TempleReady disk. I took it to the family file desk at the Jordan River Temple and got the cards printed off for the work. Although I carried Wendla's card with me every week when I went to the temple to play the organ in the baptistery chapel, I procrastinated doing her baptism. One day, toward the end of my shift, it came into my mind that I should do Wendla's baptism. I went to get my baptismal clothes, and the most wonderful feeling came over me. I found myself crying—that joyful kind of crying that is a witness of the Spirit. I was absolutely taken aback. When I got into the font and the baptizer raised his right hand and spoke Wendla's name, again I couldn't hold back the tears. I knew Wendla was accepting that baptism and was rejoicing over it.

In the fifty-something years since her death, she had obviously been busy on the other side, learning the gospel and applying its principles. Now she was eager and ready for her work to be done. I was greatly humbled that I had misjudged this dear woman.

When I did Wendla's initiatory, the feeling was even stronger. Both the worker and I were overcome with the Spirit and had to pause to get control of our emotions. The worker said that she had never felt a presence so strongly. I not only felt Wendla's presence, but I also felt her joy. I knew that she was there, had been anxiously waiting for this day, and was grateful to me for being her proxy. It was the most joyous temple experience of my entire life. A bond of love was created between Wendla and me that I can feel to this day. I rarely think of her without a swelling of the Spirit in my breast.

What Greater Witness?

The implications of that experience were enormous. I was raised in the Church, served a mission, married the first time in the temple, had always been active, and always had a testimony. But never had I received a stronger validation of the truthfulness of the gospel than through that experience. Never had I received a more sure witness of the reality of the spirit world, or the importance of temple work, or of the bright and beautiful light of truth that was restored by Elijah to the prophet Joseph.

When I returned home and shared that experience with Doug, I felt the Spirit's witness again as I spoke. The implications were not lost on him, and a few months later, he surprised me by bringing home a temple recommend. I had waited for that day for more than a decade. He received his own endowment and did the work for both of his great-grandfathers and his great-uncle. Since then, we have done temple work for many more of his ancestors, and we continue to find information on his various lines. We have grown closer as a couple through our calling to help others with this work, spending time helping them during our shifts at the multistake library.

Extended Blessings

Little did I realize how much I was going to need the added strength these experiences gave me. In September of 2004, three years after I did Wendla's work, my second son, Brian, took his own life. We had known that he was struggling with depression, but we had no idea that he suffered from bipolar disorder.

Though Brian had left the Church at the age of sixteen and had made many choices that brought him grief, he was a fine person in so many ways—gracious, kind, honest, generous. I loved him dearly and had always anguished over his problems.

My experience with Wendla and my study of the scriptures—especially Doctrine and Covenants 134—have given me much comfort and hope in the aftermath of Brian's death. I know that the dead who repent will be redeemed. I know that Wendla had the gospel preached to her in its purity and power, that she accepted it and repented, and that she accepted her temple work. What a great tutoring precedent for the situation I faced last year.

My son is now included in my "loved ones who have gone before," and he is inspiring and influencing me now in many ways. I'm grateful that we can soon do his temple endowment work, and I have great hope that he will accept it. I am grateful for my husband's continuing comfort and support in this situation, and grateful that we can now attend the temple together.

It seems that the blessings of that small effort to do Wendla's work are never-ending in my life. I feel certain that she will now be working on the other side of the veil to help Doug and me as we strive to find more information about her ancestors. I bear witness that family history work has brought me more feelings of peace and joy than I could ever have anticipated.

Letter to Mei-Li

by Mark W. Hannig

*W*hen a couple is left childless, one solution in our wonderful culture is to adopt homeless children, bring them up in righteousness, and seal them to the family. There is no question that these children are every bit as much members of their families as birth children. They are part of the family that is "found."

In this poignant essay, an uncle, who has himself been adopted into the Hannig family, writes a beautiful letter to his new seventeen-month-old Chinese niece, Mei-Li Frances Hannig, who has recently arrived from China and—in the temple of the Lord—takes her permanent place in the family with her wonderful American parents, grandparents, and extended family.

The precious process of adoption ("found" family members) brings home in an especially tender way the beauty of sealing our loved ones to us. Accepting with gratitude and affection these ordinances is one of the highlights in the lives of all of us.

My Dear Mei-Li:

This morning you sat on an altar, upstairs in a Manti Temple sealing room, your hand touching those of your adopted father and mother. You wore a white dress with a close and stiff collar, the silk reflecting translucent sunlight pouring through the windows above and bouncing off the mirrors that surrounded us.

In those mirrors I saw your two grandmothers who helped to steady you on the altar. Your two grandfathers witnessed your sealing to my brother and his wife. Faces of your aunts and uncles,

158

and your great-aunts and great-uncles shone in those mirrors. Cousins appeared too.

As the gentleman conducting the ceremony began, tears welled up in my eyes and I let them trickle down my cheeks as I am prone to do. Even at my age, I fancy myself the stoic warrior depicted in the television commercials of my childhood, who remains ready for battle in defense of his homeland, but always has a tender heart for his tribe's little ones. Perhaps I wept as much for my own joy as I did for yours. Like you, as an adopted baby, I once sat on an altar upstairs in a temple sealing room, my hand on those of my new father and mother—your paternal grandparents.

Watching you, I felt warmed by the fire of the glowing stories of our ancestors who are sealed to us—and we to them—by the power of the priesthood. I pray that our stories and our ancestors will wrap their arms around you, sing their lullabies to you, and that you may sleep deeply in their watch. I hope you feel safe enough to want to learn these stories and tell them to your children. I hope your children will learn these stories, and maybe even unearth some stories of our ancestors that they can teach to me.

When she was still living on this earth, I spoke with your father's mother's mother—your great-grandmother Mary. She told me of her life in South Carolina, where her family worked on a dairy farm. She told me how she and her brothers and sisters would walk past the farm owner's house—a large white home off-limits to them—and how she wondered what life would be like if she could just have a bicycle like the farm owner's children did. She told me about your great-grandfather, her husband, Edgar. Before they were married Edgar suffered from what psychiatrists today might call "depression." However, the country doctor back then prescribed a country remedy: work. The doctor told Edgar to wheelbarrow a big pile of rocks back and forth across the barnyard several times a day for several days in a row. Edgar did. According to Mary, the medicine took and the depression broke. Mary told me about her most wrenching challenge: defying her father (your great-great-grandfather) by becoming a Mormon and marrying one to boot. In those times and in that place, Mary crossed a line that most young women would not or could not have brought themselves to do.

I don't know exactly why, but Mary confided some of these stories to me, a grandchild, but never had told them to her own children. She might have needed the time and space to reflect about those stories. I might have been the first one to ask. Who knows? Whatever the reason, I hope you learn through my experience: your grandparents may tell you things that they have never told your dad or me. So please seek out your grandparents' stories. Warm yourself by their fire. Then come share your warmth with us and tell us the stories you have learned. Tell them to your children.

Your paternal grandfather's people also tell stories that warm and boost courage. Your grandfather's great-grandmother is Karen Jensen Neilson Hannig, born August 27, 1846, in Horsens, Vejle, Denmark. She joined the LDS Church and met and married Fredrick August Julius, a Prussian who could speak seven languages. Karen gave birth to her first child in Denmark, your great-great-grandfather. Then Karen left the company of her parents and, with her husband, set sail for America and the Saints in Utah. She bore her second child in Provo. Then Karen and Fredrick were called to live in the Dixie mission, where Fredrick could put to use his Old-World craftsmanship and help establish the cotton mills in Washington County, Utah. He died in 1892. Karen was left a widow at age forty-six with seven children to rear. She scratched and saved. To make ends meet, she worked in the cotton mills that she and Fredrick had helped to found. She died on April 24, 1929, having spent thirty-seven years as a widow in a frontier town.

Mei-Li, I hope that these stories and these women who are your foremothers give you hope, courage, and comfort. I hope that as you face your own challenges that you will look to these people for guidance. Along with many others, I hope they will provide you with a sense that you are a part of a family that extends eternally, beyond your immediate self. You will bring your own stories, your struggles, and your joys to our family's stage. The drama, tragedy, and comedy of your life may resemble mine in a few points. We are both adopted into this family. Like me, in times of preteen angst you may wrestle to know that you really belong. In other points, your trials may differ from mine. You were born several decades after me and you were born in China.

Regardless of your personal trials, I hope that you feel close enough to feel our family's warmth. If Mary and Karen could face what they did, you should be able to succeed with what life brings your way. I believe that they, along with many others of our fore-bears, look upon us and want the best for us. We are sealed to them. They want us to be happy.

May you have much health, happiness, and prosperity.

Love, Your Uncle,

Mark W. Hannig

Discovering Family Treasures

by Don Marshall

$\mathcal{W}$ho says looking into family history is tedious business? I spent most of my life in the excitement of pursuing the arts—film, drama, literature, painting—and for many years I thought that genealogy was just "for other people." But the more I have dipped into family history, the more I have realized that the love I have always had for the arts certainly didn't just begin with me.

One of the first discoveries I made was that a sense of humor and whimsy has run in my family for many years. Relatives of my mother—Otis and Mariah—had, for most of their adult lives, been dubbed "Uncle Oats" and "Aunt Rye." And my mother's first cousin was not only named Julius Caesar Riding, but he actually ended up marrying a Cleopatra Hall. (Something that has not ended there, since my latest granddaughter was just recently named—with a smile as well as much respect—Cleopatra.)

As I have continued my research, I have been most impressed to learn how my fascination with drama—whether on the stage or in film—must have come through my genes. My maternal grandfather, I've learned, spent his whole life in theater and entertainment. Here I was all these years, singing and tap dancing in programs and on TV from four to fourteen, awarded best actor in high school, and winning prizes for musical productions—especially for the musical version of my book, *The Rummage Sale*—and it was only later in life that I really began to understand how much as a professional performer my grandfather had been immersed in acting and singing as well.